JEAN HUON

THE M 16

CASEMATE
Havertown, PA

CASEMATE

2114 Darby Road
Havertown, PA 19083

Tel (610) 853-9131
Fax (610) 853-9146

www.casematepublishing.com

Translated from the French by Sheila Farnsworth

ISBN 1-932033-25-4

Originally published in France by Éditions Crépin-Leblond 2002

Thanks to the following for their help with this English version of the book:
Mr. Michael R. Farnsworth, Mr. Kenneth S. Gallagher, Mr. Ken Grapes

PUBLISHER'S NOTE

The reader will quickly notice that we have chosen to use the metric system of measurements in almost all instances. This was done deliberately to ensure complete accuracy in translating the text and information boxes from the original French. There are many resources available to provide the interested reader with metric / imperial measurement conversions.

Printed in the European Union by Estudios Graficos Zure, Spain

In Memory of Eugene Stoner
(1922-1997)

Inventor of the M 16

Eugene Stoner (1922-1997)
Photo Armalite Inc

THE INVENTOR

THE INVENTOR

Eugene Stoner was born in Gasport, Indiana in 1922.

After studying in Long Beach, California he worked for Vegas Aircraft, which later became the Lockheed Corporation.

During World War II he served with the US Marine Corps in the South Pacific and Northern China theaters of operations.

At the end of the war he left the Marine Corps and took up civilian life as an inventor, developing numerous light arms, such as the AR-3, AR-7, AR-10, AR-5/M 16 and AR-18 for the Armalite company, then the Stoner 63 Arms System.

Stoner's career as an inventor took off and he registered more than one hundred patents on various types of arms.

At the end of the Cold War he met Mikhail Kalashnikov the famous Soviet arms designer.

Towards the end of his life he collaborated with the Knight Manufacturing Company in the development of the SR-25 sharp shooter.

He died of cancer in 1997 at his home in Palm City, Florida.

Foreword

Jean Huon is one of Europe's leading firearms specialists and has written and contributed to numerous books on the subject.

Here he turns his expert attention to one of the most famous weapons produced since World War 2. The M 16 has had many admirers since its first introduction and has been manufactured in enormous quantities.

This book provides an unprecedented visual feast of information on this important firearm, from its initial development and the prototypes that preceded it to its most current version.

Along the way Jean Huon examines countless varients of the weapon and the countries which have taken it up. In addition there is an enormous amount of detailed techincal information on each of the versions of the weapon.

American Infantry Firearms in the 1950s	9
Armalite Inc.	17
The M 16	25
The M 16 A1	31
The M 16 A2	39
Long-barreled derivatives of the M 16	45
Short-barreled M 16s	51
Grenade launchers	61
Machine-gun versions of the M 16	69
The M 16 as a sharpshooter's rifle	75
The M 16 as submachine gun	81
Accessories for the M 16	85

CONTENTS

Summary tables of Colt variants of the M 16	107
M 16s produced under license	117
Copies and derivatives of the M 16	123
Users of the M 16 or its derivatives	129
The .22 Long Rifle conversions	137
Recreational use copies of the M 16	141
US 5.56 mm ammunition	147
After the M 16 A2…	151
Epilogue	156
Bibliography	158
Acknowledgements	159

American infantry firearms in the 1950's

The Unites States was the first country in the world to equip its entire army with semi-automatic firearms. In 1936 the weapon adapted by John Garand, the M 1 rifle, was introduced. This weapon was used during the Second World War and the Korean War by the majority of US soldiers. It was also used widely across five continents by America's allies.

In addition to the M 1, the old Springfield magazine rifle was brought back into service during the course of the Second World War, primarily for training purposes and also for equipping certain specific units such as the Military Police. A cheaper version known as the M 1903 A 3 was produced. This was used in combat, particularly by the US Marine Corps in the Pacific Theater.

Other weapons such as the Thompson sub-machine gun were put into service. The Thompson was produced in a variety of forms, the last of which, the model M 1 A 1, was widely used in battle. Powerful, robust and efficient, its drawbacks were its weight and the high cost of manufacture. At the end of the war it was replaced by a much more basic model, the M 3, made of stamped and soldered parts with a minimum of machine tooling. This in turn led to a simplified version, the M 3 A 1, which was in use right up to the First Gulf War.

The separate development and use of rifles and sub-machine guns continued for many years within the weaponry of all the armies in the world. However, the appearance of the M 1 carbine during the Second World War should not be forgotten.

This was at first intended to replace the pistol among non-combatants and Special Forces. However, it quickly became very popular because of its light weight, its precision, its ease of handling and, it must be said, its shape. In spite of reduced effectiveness caused by the use of relatively poor ammunition, this carbine rapidly became the principal weapon of many

Long barrelled weapons used by US troops and their allies during the Second World War.

From top to bottom:

- *Springfield M 1903 repeater 5-round weapon firing .30-06 (7.62 x 63).*
- *Springfield M 1903 A3 repeater.*
- *Garand M 1 semi-automatic fed by a clip of eight .30-06 cartridges.*
- *M 1 Carbine semi-automatic with 15-round magazine. Fires a short .30 M1 carbine cartridge (7.62 x 33).*
- *M 1 A1 Carbine with folding buttstock.*

Photo Jean Huon

Light arms ammunition used by the USA during the Second World War and the Korean War.
From left to Right
.30-06
.30 Carbine
.45 ACP
Photo Jean Huon

front line troops in 1942. In 1943 a carbine with a folding butt was produced for airborne troops. This was the M 1 A 1.

In 1944 a model fitted with a selector was added to the original two versions – the M 2 carbine. Ever since the adoption of the carbine the possibility of firing in bursts had been envisaged but it had never been realized. The idea returned with the M 2 when it became possible to equip the weapon with a 30-round magazine.

Even before the end of the war the authorities had considered adapting the Garand by fitting it with a selector and so giving it the same fire power with which the Germans had been able to equip their troops, by making an assault rifle capable of firing an intermediate cartridge. But

it turned out not to be so simple. Various attempts by Springfield and by Remington were dragged out not only by a lack of investment but also by indecision on the part of the military authorities of the day.

After the war Springfield Arsenal continued development work with varying degrees of success, in the course of which, they thought of adopting a new kind of ammunition which could be considered as an intermediate cartridge, and which could be brought into NATO-wide service.

They first investigated using .280 (7mm) caliber ammunition but then went back to 7.62mm, with two versions: the British .280/.30 (7.62 x 44) and the American T 65 E2 (7.62 x 51), which were adopted by the countries of NATO and

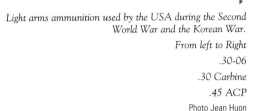

Thompson M 1 A1 machine pistol. A heavy but robust weapon. Equipped with a selector. Remains extremely precise in single shot fire.

> *Caliber: 11.43 mm*
> *Ammunition: .45 ACP*
> *Total length: 0.613 meter*
> *Barrel length: 0.267 meter*
> *Weight without magazine: 4.750 kg*
> *Magazine capacity: 20 or 30 rounds*
> *Rate of fire: 700 rounds / minute*

Photo Jean Huon

Lighter but more basic, the M 3 A1 has no selector.
Its shape and its metal plate construction gave it
the 'Grease Gun' nickname …
Caliber: 11.43 mm
Ammunition: .45 ACP
Total length: 0.754 meter
Length with buttstock retracted: 0.580 meter
Barrel length: 0.203 meter
Weight without magazine: 4.650 kg
Magazine capacity: 30 rounds
Rate of fire: 350/450 rounds / minute
Photo Jean Huon

many others, and called the 7.62mm NATO. All that remained was to decide which particular weapon would be used to fire this new ammunition. Although NATO finally managed to agree about ammunition it was a very different matter when it came to the rifle.

The Benelux countries (Belgium, Holland and Luxembourg), Great Britain and Canada opted for the FAL made by the Fabrique Nationale de Herstal in Belgium but the USA had different ideas. After long discussions on the advantages and disadvantages of the FAL (which was known in the US as the T 48) and the T 44, the military authorities decided in favor of a home-produced rifle.

The new American assault rifle, adopted in 1957 as the M 14, was an improved version of the Garand. A shorter trigger-guard released the barrel, which was fitted with a muzzle brake. The gas cylinder was also shorter. A more compact breech casing held a breech block which locked with a helical movement. A ballbearing reduced the friction between the bolt and the working parts. The feed was from a magazine. With all these characteristics the M 14 was a tough, precise and reliable weapon so long as it was used as a semi-automatic. Used as an automatic it became cranky, imprecise and very difficult for even a strong man to control. To avoid a useless waste of ammunition the selector was often locked in the semi-automatic position in the armory.

Production of the M 14 began in 1957 and ended in 1963. A total of 1,380,346 of this type were produced.

M 14 Assault rifle, single weapon with selector.
Fires a 7.62mm NATO cartridge fed by a box magazine.
Ammunition: 7.62 mm NATO (or .30 NATO)
Total Length: 1.120 meter
Barrel length: 0.560 meter
Weight without magazine: 3.700 kg
Magazine capacity: 20 rounds
Rate of fire: 750 rounds / minute
Photo U.S. Army

US soldier firing the M 14
Photo U.S. Army

In spite of studies undertaken at that time on the development of the 7.62mm NATO assault weapon, and in spite of the M 14's coming into service, it was clear that for certain parts of the US Army this weapon was still not the best choice. At the request of the Infantry Board at Fort Benning, the Continental Army Command (CONARC) worked, from 1957 onwards, on a new family of infantry weapons with fire control selection.

The specifications for these weapons were as follows:
- maximum loaded weight equal to or less than 3 kilograms;
- precision and trajectory at least equal to those of the Garand at 500 meters;
- the ammunition to be able to penetrate light armor and the energy remaining at 500m to be able to pierce a heavy helmet;
- the stopping power at 500m equal to or superior to the .30 Carbine cartridge.

Although there was no particular specification for the caliber and the cartridge, the principal manufacturers knew pretty well what was required.

The two cartridges chosen after NATO trials. Left the .280/.30. Right the .30 T65 E2.
Photo Jean Huon

The M 16

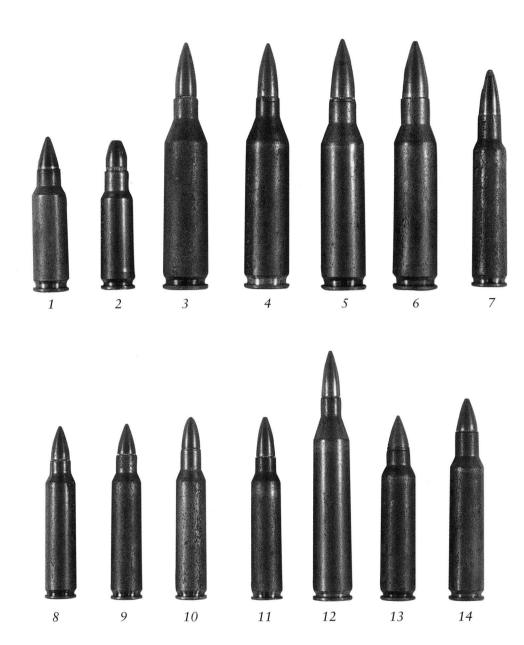

This illustrates the evolution of US small caliber cartridges between 1953 and 1959

1 - .22 Carbine, made by Winchester from 1954 to 1956 using swaged and shortened .222 Remington cases, and not from the .30 Carbine. Tested on modified M 1 carbines at the Aberdeen Proving Ground. Not retained, as its performance was judged inadequate.

2 - 5.7mm MMJ. .30 M 1 case swaged to 5.57mm, developed by Melvin M. Johnson at the beginning of the fifties. It was intended for the M 1 carbine. Offered to the military authorities in 1963 but not retained. Followed by a civilian version sold under the name of Johnson Spitfire.

3, 4, 5 & 6 - Group of four cartridges named the "Homologous Series", produced by swaging the neck of the .30 FAT 1 E 3 (the future 7.62 NATO) case. Produced by Olin Industries between 1953 and 1956. Cases marked WCC. They are:

- .18 caliber with 2.24gm base (Vo = 1 293 ms) mounted on case dated between 1953 and 1956.

- 22 caliber named the .22 T 65 by Winchester (and also .22 NATO). Trialed with T 44 and T 47 carbines. Several types of charge were tested: 3.46 bullet double charged (2 projectiles of 2.24gm or 2.26gm). Speeds ranging from 990 to 1200 meters per second.

- 25 caliber, cases dated 1953-56.

- 27 caliber, same period. The .25 and .27 (and doubtless also the .18) were tested on rebored Winchester M 70 carbines

7 - .224 Springfield (5.6 x 47), developed for a rifle of the same period as the Winchester and the Armalite.

8 - .224 Winchester E 1. Developed after 1955-56.

9 - .224 Winchester E 2. Tested in 1958. Used with the light Winchester rifle

10 - .222 Remington Magnum. Produced in 1957 under military contract. Initially designated .22 Caliber Experimental. Rejected by the military. Later formed part of the Remington sporting range under the name .222 Remington Magnum.

11 - .222 Special. Initial designation of the .223 Remington. First produced in 1957. Examples marked .223 date from 1962 (WCC) and 1963 (REM).

12 - .30/.22 Produced at the Frankford Arsenal in 1957, with a 5.5 caliber ball mounted on a .30-06 case with swaged neck. Sometimes found wrongly named '.22-06'.

13 - .25 Winchester (6.35 x 47.7). Found with cases marked WCC 58 or FA 59. Designated FAT 110 by Frankford Arsenal, the case was named FAT 116 and the double charge FAT 115.

14 - .25 caliber (6.35 x 52.8). Case marked FA 59 and designated FAT 125. The single ball has the reference number FAT 114 and the double FAT 127.

Photo Jean Huon

◄

Light Winchester rifle produced in 1958 in response to the CONARC program

Caliber: .224

Total length: 0.955 meter

Barrel length: 0.508 meter

Loaded Weight: 2.490 kg

Magazine capacity: 20 rounds

Photo Winchester

Since 1953 the US Army had been interested in small caliber ammunition, which had been around for several years in the form of hunting cartridges, and at the end of its project CONARC put out a call to all firms capable of developing a light assault weapon and its ammunition.

Only two firms responded positively to CONARC's request: Winchester and Armalite. Winchester offered a light automatic rifle developed by Ralph Clarckson. This had a number of features found in the M 2 carbine:
• gas blowback operation;
• moving breech with helical locking;
• fire selector.

This weapon used .224 Winchester E 1 ammunition weighing 3.4gm (Vo=1000 m/s, Eo=170 kg). Stress was laid on its light weight, evidenced by its construction: breech casing and magazine were made in light alloy and the barrel was grooved externally.

The Armalite Company, to which we shall return in the next chapter, offered the AR-11 carbine, which was characterized by a specialized blowback system, a closed breech casing and a locked bolt with multiple lugs. The manufacturers had, to a large extent, used light alloys and plastics in its construction. It fired a .221 Remington bullet with a dual-coned 3.5 gm tip. The slug had been conceived by Eugene

The M 16

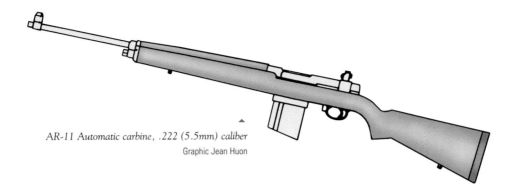

AR-11 Automatic carbine, .222 (5.5mm) caliber

Graphic Jean Huon

Stoner and its manufacture had been entrusted to Sierra Bullets, but the proposed weapon proved less than satisfactory because it remained too unstable in automatic fire mode.

Finally it was decided to go ahead with a modified version of the AR-10 (a 7.62 NATO assault rifle) which was named as the AR-15. This counter-bored weapon, like the .221 Remington, proved well-adapted to firing in bursts, mainly because the stock was aligned with the barrel. CONARC put in an order for ten AR-15's plus 100 magazines.

The Winchester .224 was set the same standards and so the two weapons found themselves in competition with each other.

It would have been possible to find a third contender: the T 44 E 6 from Springfield, a .224 weapon developed from the M 14 by A. J. Lizza, but it was never submitted for trial.

Before moving on to the M 16 itself it is only right that we examine the Armalite Company and explain the stages which led to the production of the AR-15.

The US had already tested a small caliber weapon in 1895. At that time many countries (including Germany, France and Sweden) were showing interest in very small caliber ammunition.

The Lee Navy Rifle was a manual repeater with a straight-line movement breech. It fired a USN 6mm cartridge whose 7.25gm shot had an initial velocity of 800 meters/second.

Photo Jean Huon

A precursor: Armalite Inc.

In 1950 George Sullivan, an American technician with Lockheed Aircraft International, came up with the idea of applying new methods to arms manufacture, mainly using non-ferrous metals and high-resistance plastics. He had had the opportunity to examine these closely because of his studies on the patents of aeronautical materials. He announced his projects to Richard Boutelle, president of the Fairchild Engine and Airplane Corp. of Hagerstown, MD. Boutelle succeeded in convincing the members of his board of the opportunities which this new activity would offer and on October 1, 1954 the Armalite Division of Fairchild was born and set up in Los Angeles, California.

Its C.E.O. was Charles Dorchester and the new firm engaged Eugene Stoner as head of research. Stoner, an ex-marine, had already made his mark by his own research into armament materials.

The carbine in transport mode.
Photo Jean Huon

The initial project was to make Armalite a business concentrating on the production of sporting weapons and competition arms but, as we shall see, their activities also turned towards military matters.

Every model projected or manufactured by Armalite was designated by the letters AR followed by a serial number. Certain weapons were made in series and in most cases their manufacture was guaranteed by the firms which had acquired the license.

AR-1 'Parasniper'

The creation of this repeating rifle goes back to 1954. It was a development based on a mechanism of the Mauser F.N. rifle on which was mounted a 7.62mm NATO barrel. The tube was made from aluminum alloy with steel armatures and it ended in a muzzle brake. The short stock, with a Monte Carlo butt, cheek rest and pistol grip, was made of fiberglass. It had a telescopic sight.

Only ten examples of the AR-1 were ever made and, in spite of its much-reduced weight (2.5kg including the sight), no series was ever manufactured.

AR-3

This semi-automatic rifle was the result of work done by Eugene Stoner before he joined Armalite. No doubt the inventor cherished the idea of offering it to the military as a possible contender in the race which would end with the adoption of the M 14.

George Sullivan (left) and Charles Dorchester (right) co-founders of Armalite Inc. George Sullivan holds a prototype hunting rifle and Charles Dorchester has two AR-5s. In front of them is a 7.62mm NATO assault rifle, the AR-16.
Photo Armalite Inc.

The AR-3 was manufactured to make use of .30 T 65 (the future 7.62mm NATO) ammunition, its shape being somewhat reminiscent of the US M 1 carbine. It operated by borrowed gas under the barrel. Its light alloy frame contained a moving assembly with locked bolt and multiple lugs. The mount was fiberglass.

The AR-3 never went beyond the prototype stage but certain of its characteristics were to reappear on later models.

AR-5

In 1955, at the request of the U.S. Air Force, Armalite looked at the possibility of a light .22 Hornet survival weapon to replace the models which were then in service. After various experiments about ten prototypes were tested under the supervision of Colonel Burton T. Miller, director of the project on behalf of the U.S.A.F. The AR-5 was a repeater. It had a locking breech bolt, a removable barrel made of aluminum alloy and a fiberglass stock. The magazine was stainless steel. The rifle was named the MA-1 but it never went into production because the U.S. Air Force. changed its mind, judging that there were sufficient M 4 survival weapons (armed with the .22 Hornet) and M 6's (with .410 Magnum and .22 Hornet together) then in service and so they backed out of the contract.

A Dutch marine testing the AR-10
Artillerie-Inrichtingen

After being manufactured by Armalite for several years the AR-7 was subsequently produced by Charter Arms of Stratford, Connecticut after 1973.

The problem was that a survival arm, essentially meant for sport, had never been a formal requirement of the US armed forces.

AR-9

This was a prototype semi-automatic hunting rifle. Its barrel and frame were light alloy weighing 2.5kg. It used a magazine clip with two cartridges, which gave three shots including the one in the chamber.

AR-10

This was a Eugene Stoner assault rifle. The plans for it were already in existence before he joined the Armalite team. These plans called for a weapon firing .30 - .60 ammunition with an F.M. BAR magazine. The single-tube barrel and stock were placed in the same axis, with the sighting mechanism immediately above them. The gas cylinder is parallel to the barrel and is located on the side. The bolt lock operates by means of multiple lugs placed at the head.

AR-7 Long Rifle .22 carbine

Photo Jean huon

AR-7 'Explorer'

Manufactured 1959 - 1960, based on a Stoner design, this model was a semi-automatic carbine firing .22 Long Rifle ammunition.

It was unusual because it was entirely constructed of water-resistant materials. Its stainless steel barrel was cased in a light alloy sleeve. The magazine and the breech block were also stainless steel. The plastic stock had a removable butt plate. This gave access to a housing where it was possible, after disassembly, to put the barrel, the breech casing and the magazine.

The whole thing, thus treated, was unsinkable.

Another variant of the prototype AR-10, assault rifle version.
Photo Armalite Inc.

It is difficult not to find certain features in common between this weapon and the M 1944 Johnson machine gun, in particular the stock, the sighting mechanism and the bolt locking system.

The second prototype, made in 1955, fired 7.62mm NATO bullets with a light alloy magazine. The triangular stock was always positioned on the axis of the barrel. The rear and front metal sights gave place to a German ZF 41 optical sight (as used in the K 98k and the G 41). A significant gain, compared with the preceding weapon, was achieved by using a dished plate.

AR-10 A

This third model is already very characteristic of the family of assault rifles of which the outcome would be the M 16. The evolution, compared with the second prototype, was achieved by modifying the frame and returning to traditional sighting mechanisms. The rear sight was placed on a support, which could

▲

AR-10A Assault Rifle.
Photo Armalite Inc.

serve as a carrying handle. The winged foresight is placed on two independent lugs on the muzzle brake flash suppressor found at the end of the barrel. The latter is of aluminum with titanium armatures recalling the experiences of the AR-1.

During 1956 the AR-10 was given intensive publicity and was offered to the US military authorities. Some flaws resulted in the weapon being altered.

AR-10 B

On this model the gas cylinder was placed above the muzzle. The muzzle brake flash suppressor was modified. The cocking lever, which had at first been fitted to the right, was now placed under the frame like an axial hook and was protected by the carrying handle.

The forward sight had moved back slightly and was now found between the handguard and the flash suppressor. An automatic opening flap sealed the ejection port as it did on the German MP 44.

▲

AR-10B Assault Rifle.
Photo Armalite Inc.

The barrel of the AR-10 B was made of extruded aluminum alloy with steel armatures. This had certain advantages, notably a 40% gain in weight, its cooling ability which was three times faster than a steel barrel, and it was also less affected by vibration.

But it had one major disadvantage: the coefficient of expansion of the barrel and its steel armature was not the same and this led to serious bias in automatic fire when the metal reached a temperature of up to 600°. Subsequent models were of 100% steel construction reserving light alloy for the frame.

The butt and the handguard were made of molded plastic strengthened with fiberglass.

It appears that when Armalite offered its AR-10 B to the US Army it was still in need of some work. Springfield Arsenal had worked for twelve years to bring out its assault weapon derived from the Garand. Many other weapons were tested and it seems that the US Army, under

"Chuck" Dorcheste and Eugene Stoner after tests on the AR-10B

Photo Armalite Inc.

pressure to make a decision and to make up for its delay, would choose to make the one for which it already had part of the ordnance, namely the Garand-derived M 14.

Armalite had also come up with a weapons system on the lines of the basic mechanism of the AR-10:

- assault rifle
- sharpshooter with telescopic sight
- short-barreled automatic rifle
- light machine gun with interchangeable barrel and belt feed

It was proposed to offer the AR-10 for export and interest was shown by the Netherlands who were able to make it under license in exchange for the production of a Fokker mechanism to be made by Fairchild.

In 1957 the state arsenal, Artillerie-Inrichtingen of Hembrug-Zaandam in Holland acquired the license.

Production began on a small scale and demonstrations were given across the world.

The market was confined to specialized firms in the arms trade:

- Cooper-MacDonald of Baltimore, USA for the far east countries in the Pacific area
- Interarmco of Alexandria, USA for Latin America
- Sidem of Bonn, Germany for Europe and Africa

Numerous countries tested the AR-10, which came out in a number of versions but, following the refusal of the Dutch government to use it to equip their armed forces, relations between the Dutch and Armalite deteriorated and the co-operation ended in 1960.

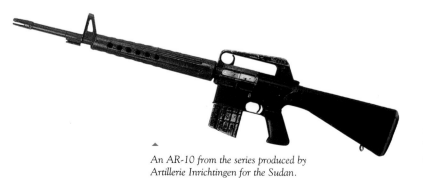

An AR-10 from the series produced by Artillerie Inrichtingen for the Sudan.

Photo Jean Huon

Sudan would have ordered between 1500 and 1800 AR-10s.
Photo Jean Huon

Artillerie-Inrichtingen produced fewer than ten thousand AR-10s, which were sold to Burma, to Guatemala (350 were bought for the Military Academy), to Portugal (1500 for the colonial troops in Angola and Mozambique) and to Sudan (1500 – 1800), plus a small number of samples for Cuba, South Africa, Germany, Austria, Finland and a few other countries. In January 1959 Armalite entrusted the AR-10 license to the Colt Patent Manufacturing Company of Hartford, CT

AR-10 Assault Rifle
Caliber: 7.62 mm
Ammunition: 7.62 mm NATO (7.62 x 51)
Total length: 1.033 meter
Barrel length: 0.510 meter
Weight with magazine empty: 3.620 kg
Magazine capacity: 20 rounds
Rate of fire: 700 rounds / minute
Photo Jean Huon

AR-11

This was a prototype light assault gun based on a model similar to the AR-3, chambered for a bullet derived from the .22 Remington. It was offered to the Infantry General Staff so that they

Photograph from an introductory booklet on the AR-10. It is being tested by a Dutch marine landing force.
Foreground: heavy version with a bipod and sighting rule for grenade firing.
Beyond: sniper version with telescopic sight.
Document Artillerie-Inrichtingen

could evaluate the advantages of very small caliber weapons. It was in competition against the light Winchester .224.

AR-15

The AR-11 was clearly not what was required and it was decided to make a reduced version of the AR-10 chambered for .22 bullets.

The result was the AR-15, which was to become the M 16 whose world-wide use is the subject of this book.

AR-16

Between 1956 and 1960 the AR-16 was an assault rifle firing 7.62mm NATO bullets. Its performance was equal to that of the AR-10 but its construction was simpler and more economical because it was stamped and welded.

The AR-16 was never produced in any number.

AR-17

This was a 12-bore automatic hunting rifle, which benefited from the progress made by Armalite in military weapons materials:

Portugal had 1500 AR-10s used by colonial troops in Angola and Mozambique.
Document Artillerie-Inrichtingen

• almost wholly made of light alloy
• multiple lug bolt locked breech

It was gradually developed between 1956 and 1962. In 1964 Armalite put a small number of AR-17s on the market but their success was limited by their high cost.

AR-18

Recognizing the advantages of light assault weapons, Armalite decided, in 1963, to produce a variation of the AR-16 using .223 Remington ammunition, with adjustments by Charles Dorchester, Arthur Miller and George Sullivan. It

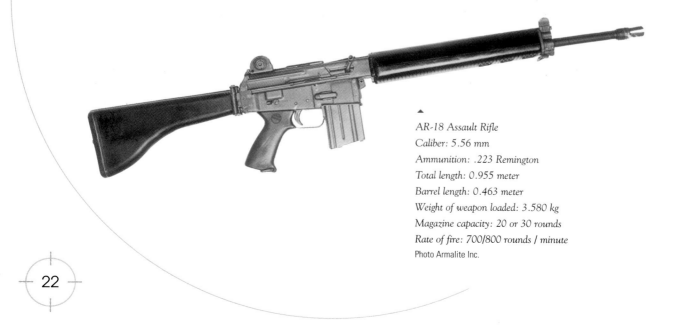

AR-18 Assault Rifle
Caliber: 5.56 mm
Ammunition: .223 Remington
Total length: 0.955 meter
Barrel length: 0.463 meter
Weight of weapon loaded: 3.580 kg
Magazine capacity: 20 or 30 rounds
Rate of fire: 700/800 rounds / minute
Photo Armalite Inc.

was a light assault rifle operated by gas blowback.

It consisted of a breech casing and a number of components in steel plate. Far fewer pieces required machining. The moving parts consisted of a moving head with seven locking lugs and two recoil springs. The butt, which could be folded laterally, was made of plastic.

The AR-18 was used in some States of the USA by the police and manufacturing licenses went abroad to:
• Howa Machinery Co. of Nagoya, Japan (1967)
• Sterling Armament Co. Ltd. of Dagenham, UK

(1976), whose products were exported to several countries, notably Botswana.

There was also an AR-18 S, stripped of its butt and having a short barrel and a second forward grip. Like the AR-180, made for civilian use, it was a single-shot weapon.

Production of the AR-18 and its derivatives was resumed in the USA in 1968.

In 1983 Armalite was sold to the Ellisco Tool Manufacturing Co. in the Philippines. This firm produced the M 16 there for the armed forces.

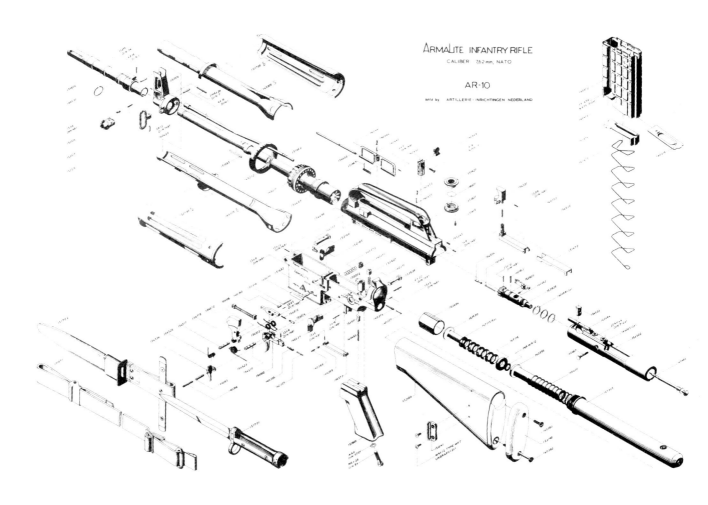

Exploded diagram of AR-10 (Portuguese version)
Document Artillerie-Inrichtingen

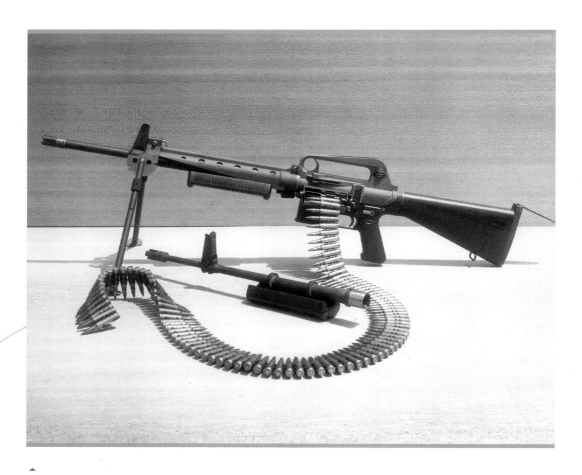

AR-10 light machine gun.
Photo Armalite Inc.

In 1986 another business, Eagle Arms, was set up at Coal Valley, Illinois.

It mass-produced spare parts and accessories for the AR-10 and the AR-15 as well as for sporting derivatives of the AR-15, sold as EA-15s.

After 1994 they remade the AR-10 and, following an agreement

- Two .50 sniper rifles, the AR-50 and AR-30
- Devices for reduced firing and blank firing for the Mk 19 automatic grenade launchers, the AR-22 and AR-23.

The AR-15 offered for trial fired a .222 (5.56 x 43) Remington cartridge while the light Winchester used a .224 E1 (which had a casing of the same length but a different profile). In the course of development it became clear that, because of the excessive pressure raised in the chamber under certain conditions (overheating of the barrel, for example) the volume of the casing would have to be increased slightly. The two companies were asked to produce a cartridge that would suit the profile of the chamber required by the US Army.

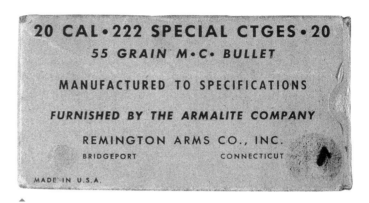

A box of .222 Remington Special cartridges made by Remington to Armalite's specification with a .55 grain (3.52gm) bullet.
Photo Jean Huon

Two trial 5.56mm versions for the US Army: on the left the .224 Winchester E2 and on the right the .222 Remington Special which was to become the .223 Remington
Photo Jean Huon

was in the usual position and the AR-15 light rifle was modified as a result. The new weapon was known as the .222 Remington Special.

The two weapons were in competition again. Their chambers had the same profile but, whereas the AR-15 could fire both the .222 Remington Special and the .224 E2, the Winchester automatic could only fire the .224 E2.

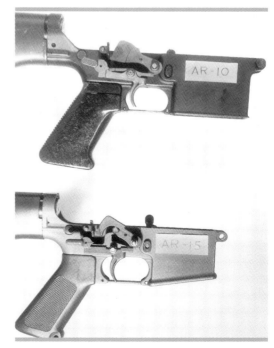

This image illustrates the differences between the mechanisms of the AR-10 and the AR-15.

The hammer locking systems are different as is the shape of the automatic firing spring
Photo Armalite Inc.

Winchester developed the .224 E2 cartridge with a 45mm casing. To make the length equal to that of the .224 E1, the New Haven company chose to recess the ball further into the collar. This arrangement was selected in order to avoid modifying the weapon itself, which would have involved a longer time-scale before it could be put into service.

At the same time Armalite asked Remington to develop a cartridge with a casing conforming to the chamber profile defined by the US Army. This casing, which had a shorter collar than that of the Winchester, was 44.5mm long. The ball

The M 16

▲
The early version of the AR-15 with honeycombed magazine, a direct descendant of the AR-10.
Photo Armalite Inc.

When the tests began it soon became clear that the AR-15 was superior to its rival as much because of the weapon itself as because of its ammunition, which became known as .223 Remington.

The AR-15 thus demonstrated that it could ultimately be the successor to the M 14 but it had first to undergo a lengthy evaluation process and this would have an important influence on the development of the M 16.

▲
The first M 16 as it was accepted by the USAF in 1963 (right side).
Photo Jean Huon

The first models were submitted to CONARC between March 20 and November 21 1958 and extensive tests were carried out at the Aberdeen Proving Ground in Maryland between September 21 and October 20, 1960. During this time three weapons were tested and a total of 24,443 rounds were fired. The result of these trials was a weighty report registered as No. DPS-96 (OMS Code No. 5530.11.559). Its salient features were as follows:

- Description of Materials,
- Detailed examination of the constituent elements,
- Removal and replacement of the stock,
- Precision firing: ten shots at 100 yards gave a standard deviation of 38mm,
- Semi-automatic fire at a practice rate of fire: 84 shots per minute were fired, of which 77 hit the target giving 92% accuracy,
- Firing in volleys: in the same conditions 128 rounds were fired giving an accuracy of 32% (41 hits),

▲

The first M 16 (left side).
Photo Jean Huon

- Precision shooting using the telescopic sight: the standard deviation was reduced to 28mm (on 10 shots at 100 yards),
- Endurance: after 18,000 shots were fired in this test only ten parts were damaged, of which one (an extractor) was damaged when being disassembled for cleaning. Misfires, at 0.25%, were relatively rare,
- Adverse conditions (frost, mud, dust, rain, salt water spray etc.),
- The hot barrel spontaneous firing test was carried out by firing a burst of 140 rounds and ignition occurred after 54 seconds.

Polar climatic tests were carried out at Fort Greely in Alaska.

After further testing at Fort Ord, California and at the Springfield Arsenal, the AR-15 underwent modifications including:

- rubber butt-plate,
- a new safety fire-control selector,
- cocking lever placed at the rear of the frame, demountable stock, muzzle brake.

There followed an order for 1000 weapons for trial with the armed forces.

But, since the Armalite Company's real function was research and development of weapons materials, it was not equipped for the production of such large numbers and in December 1959 Colt's Patent Firearms Manufacturing Co. received the manufacturing license for the AR-10 and the AR-15.

Despite the fact that Colt, through their South-East Asia agents Cooper MacDonald, won an order for 25 AR-15s for Malaysia and 10 for Indonesia, the US armed forces continued with their evaluation using fifteen different groups, representing the Army, the Air Force, the Navy and the Marine Corps.

Finally, in 1962 Colt received its first official order: 8500 AR-15s for the US Air Force (to be used by security personnel at Strategic Air Command bases) and 1000 for the Defense Department which decided to send the new weapons to Vietnam.

In 1963 the US Navy placed a limited order. In October the situation became critical and the Air Force decided to adopt the AR-15, calling it the M 16, to replace the shoulder weapons then in service (the M 14, the M 2 and the M 31 machine pistol). A first consignment of 19,000 weapons was ordered.

▲

This model still has the frame of the earlier one but without the ribbing to reinforce the feed tube. This also protects the button of the magazine lock.
Photo Jean Huon

The Army was more cautious than the Air Force, thinking long and hard before putting the new weapon into service. It still had a number of criticisms, partly justified. It brought into service a model known as the XM 16 E1, which

The M 16

◄
The new weapon first appeared during an extensive campaign in San Domingo in 1965.

Here we see a medic of the US 82nd Airborne Division (All-American) armed with what the media of the day described as 'a plastic machine gun'.

Photo U.S. Army

had a safety on the rifle bolt among other features.

This weapon was assigned as a priority to the Rangers, Special Forces and paratroopers serving in Vietnam.

84,250 were ordered in November 1963, 100 more in October 1965. Over 500,000 of these weapons were put into service before its official adoption and before it became known as the M 16 A1. It was progressively used to equip all the US armed forces with the exception of the Air Force, which kept the M 16 for some time.

In June 1967 the US Government paid Colt $4.5 million for a manufacturing license for the M 16. The Vietnam War was in full swing and tenders were invited to find sources of supply which could complete Colt's production.

In December 1968 Harrington & Richardson and the Hydra Matic Division of General Motors each received a contract for the provision of

▲
This weapon was used as a reference by the French Army during the tests which set the FAMAS, the HK 33F and the CAL against each other

Photo Jean Huon

An early M 16 with split muzzle brake in Vietnam in the Tay Ninh region about 100 km north west of Saigon (25th Infantry Division 6th April 1967).

Photo U.S. Army

240,000 M 16 A1s. The weapons had to be delivered quickly and the rate of delivery was set at 25,000 weapons per month by November 1969.

But the commitments were not adhered to, the time extensions were not respected, the quality of certain products left much to be desired and the prices were variable, to say the least:

- $104 from Colt.
- $250 from H & R.
- $316 from Hydramatic.

At this point a Government commission of inquiry began to criticize the M 16 from all directions. The inquiries multiplied and doubts were expressed about its reliability, its cost and its usefulness. Eventually things sorted themselves out and the three contractors found themselves with confirmed orders for 740,803 M 16 A1s, 1000 M 16s and the conversion of 135,001 M 16s to standard M 16 A1s.

Colt continued to manufacture the weapon both for the US and for the international market. It had already made 5,000,000 by 1975

The first M 16 A1s were delivered to South Vietnamese forces on July 31st 1969 and from the start received unanimous praise from the troops using them. Lighter than the Garand M 1, with higher performance than the US carbine, the new weapon was much valued.
Photo U.S. Army

and 8,000,000 (of all versions) by the time the M 16 A2 was adopted in 1983.

193,949 examples of the M 16 were produced between 1962 and 1965, of which 50,000 were for civilian use (by police and hunters) and for export.

Today the number of M 16s and its derivatives is in excess of ten million.

The M 16 A1

Testing the M 16 in Vietnam had enabled the US Army to make judgments about the behavior of the weapon in the field. Their conclusions were as follows:

Advantages

- Lightweight.
- Ease of handling.
- Precision.
- Extreme stability in automatic firing, even when used one-handed without a shoulder rest!
- Wounding effect of ammunition was satisfactory up to 400m
- Very appreciable perforation power of the projectile even when striking at an angle (up to 70°).
- Rust resistant

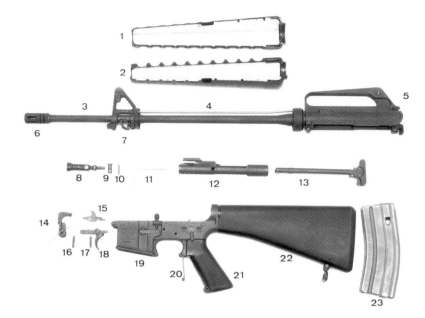

M 16 A1, older model buttstock (no housing for cleaning materials and jointed sling swivel).

Photo Colt

Disadvantages

- Strain imposed on the weapon (especially the butt) when firing grenades with fins longer than 22mm.
- Risk that the reduced caliber could retain water by capillary action and so lead to the barrel bursting.
- Easily fouled by mud or dust.

◀

Principal parts of the early M 16 A1.

Note the jointed sling swivel and the lack of serration on the breech.

Photo Colt

▲

Description of parts of the M 16 A1 (first type):

1. Left shell of handguard
2. Right shell of handguard
3. Barrel
4. Adductor tube
5. Combined breech case and carrying handle
6. Muzzle brake - flash-suppressor / grenade launcher
7. Gas-intake jacket
8. Bolt head
9. Maneuvering pin
10. Firing pin retaining spindle
11. Firing pin
12. Breech bolt
13. Cocking lever
14. Hammer and spring
15. Semi-automatic firing catch
16. Hammer spindle
17. Firing-catch spindle
18. Trigger with its spring
19. Feed tube and action housing assembly
20. Retractable trigger guard
21. Pistol grip
22. Buttstock
23. 30-round magazine

Photo Colt

The M 16

Since this last problem was by far the most serious in terms of the M 16's adoption by the US Army, a modification was introduced. This took the form of a safety catch on the breech lock, which was set obliquely behind and to the right of the frame. There were other, less critical, changes:

- Enlarged cocking lever to allow it to be used when wearing gloves.
- Small anti-fouling notches arranged on the side faces of the breech lock.
- Lighter firing pin
- Chamber and barrel chrome plated.
- Rifling reduced from 14 to 12 inches to allow the bullet to remain stable at sub-zero temperatures.
- Slower rhythm of fire due to a new shock absorber.

Second-generation M 16 A1
Photo Jean Huon

- Reinforcement of the feed tube to the level of the safety anchorage of the magazine.
- etc.

Modified in this way the M 16 became the XM 16 E1 and more than 500,000 were manufactured before its official acceptance on February 28, 1967.

Description

The front of the steel barrel was screwed into the breech casing.

It was bored to 5.56mm caliber and has right-handed rifling for 305mm. It terminates in a muzzle brake flash suppressor.
The early models of this were forked and

An M 16 A1 produced by the Hydromatic Division of General Motors
Photo Jean Huon

shaped like a truncated cone but were replaced by a cylindrical model with six slots countersunk lengthways. Two thirds of the way along the barrel were the vent hole and the gas intake jacket combined with a mounting which carried:

- above, the cross-sight.
- below, the sling swivel and the bayonet lug.

The gas cylinder was made up of a simple supply tube without a ram. Situated above the barrel, slightly offset to the right of the breech, it led directly to the face of the working part.[1]

---

[1] For some time some authors have claimed that this system had been borrowed from the Swedish semi-automatic AG 42, however, it was Rossignol, the French "contrôleur d'armes" who first applied this principle in 1896.

The direct action gas duct is used as the motor system to operate the mechanism of several prototypes of automatic and semi-automatic weapons. It is found again during the 1920s on French experimental arms, which led to the development of the MAS 40, MAS 44, MAS 49 and MAS 49-56.

The handguard which surrounded the part of the barrel between the breech casing and the gas intake ring was triangular in section, comprising two symmetrical shells of molded plastic. To improve cooling, apertures, ten above and six below, were inserted in the breech casing. Each shell was strengthened by a section of reinforced, riveted aluminum. The handguard was held in front by a triangular cup fixed to the sight support and at the rear by a spring dish fixed around the barrel just in front of the frame.

The left face of the M 16 A1 frame carries regulatory and maker's marks (Colt here). The selector and breech catch can also be seen.
Photo Jean Huon

Cartoon strip instruction manual encouraging users of the XM 16 E1 to look after the weapon correctly.
US Army document approved by Chief of Staff General W.C.Westmoreland (1969)

The Frame had two elements:
- A lower mount, made in one piece with the feed tube, locks the trigger mechanism. The latter consists of the pawl, the spring catches for automatic and semi-automatic fire, the cocking piece and their springs. The fire selector is above and to the left of the pistol grip close to the thumb. The magazine catch is to the right and can be moved by the index finger without loosening the grip. The lower section of the trigger guard can be removed (by pushing the spring-loaded spindle with the point of a bullet) so as to allow firing when wearing gloves.
- On the upper part the breech casing is cylindrical and houses the moving parts. The cocking lever is to the rear and operates over the buttstock, its T-shape allowing the weapon to be loaded both left and right handed. A small spring catch retracts as soon as the cocking lever is held; it was put there to hold the lever in the forward position and thus avoid accidental locking. The upper part of the breech casing consists of a trapezoidal knob which works as the carrying handle and carries the rear sight (or later, telescopic sight). The ejection port is situated to the right and is

The closing system consists of a button positioned to the right of the breech case. This is fitted with a retracting spring and its forward portion connects with the machined slots in the side of the breech lock.

The patent for this mechanism was registered by Foster E. Sturtevant on behalf of Colt and it was recognized on February 22nd 1966 with the number 3.263.155.
Photo Jean Huon

The M 16

The two parts which form the body are brought together by a forward sight and a rear pin, which are arranged transversely. This body is made entirely of pressure-molded and machined light alloy. The finish is anodized matt dark gray.

Type 2 portable assembly with lateral fins to assist with automatic cleaning

Finished with a phospate surfacing.

Photo Colt

The moving system consists of:
- The breech itself, which is cylindrical and hollow to allow the transit of the cocking piece, has to the front right an oblique slope holding the maneuvering pin of the mobile head.
- On top of the breech is a stamping, fixed with two Allen screws, which connects with the gas cylinder. This acts as a collector.
- The moving head carries seven interlocking splines in a star formation. The toggle extractor has one and this raises the number of locking mechanisms to eight. The fore cup has two holes, one to allow the passage of the firing pin, the other for the passage of the ejector. The trigger pin crosses the rear of the breech and also the whole of the moving head. It has no release spring.

All the moving parts of the first M 16s were cadmium plated. After that they were phosphated.

Sight of the M 16 situated above the carrying handle. It consists of a bracket with two apertures mounted on an adjustable pivot.

Photo Jean Huon

The feed was by means of two types of magazine clip, twenty shot straight or thirty shot banana shaped.

At the end of the loading clip a catch immobilized the moving head in the rear position. To retract it one had either to press the required button, found on the left face of the gear casing above the feed tube, or insert a new, full magazine.

The sighting components were as follows:
- A sight positioned on the rear of the carrying handle made up of two apertures on a tilting

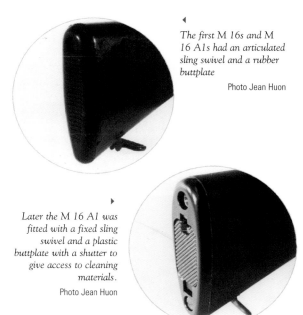

The first M 16s and M 16 A1s had an articulated sling swivel and a rubber buttplate

Photo Jean Huon

Later the M 16 A1 was fitted with a fixed sling swivel and a plastic buttplate with a shutter to give access to cleaning materials.

Photo Jean Huon

bracket. The first of these apertures was for shots of up to 300m and the second for shots of 300m - 500m. The bracket was mounted on a transverse screw allowing for deflection adjustments. It was operated by using the point of a bullet to move a perforated disc positioned to the right of the sight. To adjust the aim point to the right the disc had to be moved counter-clockwise.
- The cross sight was placed on top of the mounting on the gas intake jacket. There were also two extrusions which formed protective lugs. The cross sight could regulate height: by turning it clockwise the point of impact was raised. Each click gave a displacement of 28mm at 100m or 56mm at 200m.

The triangular butt stock, made of black, molded plastic like the stock and the pistol grip, was placed directly on the axis of the barrel. On

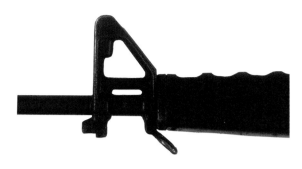

The M 16's fore-sight is fitted on the gas intake jacket. It can be adjusted for height

Photo Jean Huon

28mm at 100m or 56mm at 200m.

The triangular butt stock, made of black, molded plastic like the stock and the pistol grip, was placed directly on the axis of the barrel. On earlier models these were olive green or dark blue. Inside the butt stock was a tube, screwed into the frame and situated on the axis of the breech block. It contained the recuperator spring. The link between this spring and the moving parts was guaranteed by a cylindrical element, which was both guide pin and spring shock absorber. There were variations in the construction of this piece right from the start.

The hinged rear ring on the shoulder strap on the AR-15 and the early M 16 A1 was replaced by a fixed ring.

The XM 16 E1 had been criticized for fouling but enquiries showed that the troops had never been issued with cleaning equipment. To remedy this each man was issued with servicing equipment which was stored in the buttstock of the weapon.

This is why the rubber butt plate was replaced by a plastic one which had a ribbed flap giving

access to the cleaning kit. On November 9th 1971 Henry A. Into and John K. Jorcza, on behalf of the Colt Company, were granted the Patent No. 3.618.248 covering this new buttstock.

Preparing to fire

Place the loaded magazine in the feeder tube.

Pull the cocking lever right back and release it. The lever should not move during firing. The shutter on the ejection port opens automatically.

The breech block is closed, locked and a bullet moves into the chamber. The weapon is ready to fire.

Single shot firing

The breech is loaded by pulling the bottom lever fully back.

Photo Jean Huon

Selector in the "half" position (knob facing down). The semi-automatic fire spring catch is placed between the two parts of the trigger, which allows the cocking piece to catch on its pin.

Firing action: the firing spring releases the hammer which, driven by its spring, strikes the firing pin. Shot emission: when the ball has passed beyond the vent hole, gases penetrate

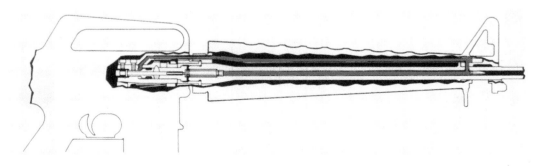

Illustration of the principle of the gas-blowbak mechanism on the M 16 A1

Document Colt

Pvt. Michael J. Mendoza of the 101st Airborne Division (Company A, 2nd Battalion, 502 PIR) fires his M 16 A1 in an area suspected of concealing a Vietcong marksman.

This incident occurred during 'Operation Cook' on September 8th 1967 in Quang Ngai Province some 500 km north east of Saigon.

Photo U.S. Army

the adductor tube and are directed towards the working parts. These gases penetrate the interior of the breech and force it to recoil. The oblique face comes into contact with the pin which holds the moving head. This makes a rotation of 22° 30′ which unlocks the breech. The moving parts recoil.

Extraction, ejection and locking the cocking piece. On compression of the recuperator spring the breech recoils into the shock absorber.

Forward movement begins: the spring expands to project in front of the breech. A new cartridge is inserted into the chamber.

Automatic Firing

Selector in 'auto' position (knob facing forward). The automatic fire spring turns slightly and holds the hammer by means of its external pin.

The firing process is the same as for single shot but the breech block frees the automatic firing spring when the firing lever is pressed.

Disassembly

Remove the magazine and follow the safety precautions.

Allow the breech to return to the forward position.

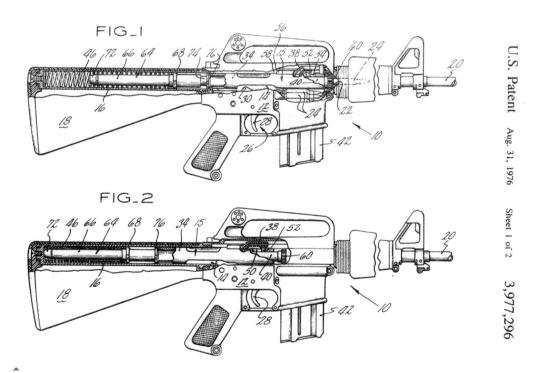

The old model shock absorber consisted of a set of elastic rings. The new model, which was fitted after 1976, had a wide tube which worked as a guide shaft for the recuperator spring. The tube had a plastic ferrule and held a piston and a shock-absorbing spring.

The illustration above, which comes from the patent document, shows in Fig.1 the shock absorber at rest. Fig.2 shows the part in its rear position at maximum compression.

This device was invented by Stanley D. Silby and Henry J Tatro.

M 16 A1 breech bolt, *head in released position.*
Photo Jean Huon

Technical Data - M 16 and M 16 A1	
Type	assault rifle
Operation	by gas blowback
Firing mode	selective
	breech closed and locked
Cooling	by air
Feed	by box-magazine
Magazine capacity	20 and 30 rounds
Caliber	5.56 mm
Ammunition	.223 Remington
Total weapon length	0.986 m
Length with bayonet	1.112 m
Barrel length	0.508 m
Barrel length with flash suppressor	0.533 m
Barrel rifling	6 to right
Twist of rifling	305 mm
Line of sight length	0.501 m
Height (without magazine)	0.224 m
Height (with 20-round magazine)	0.224 m
Height (with 30 round magazine)	0.252 m
M 16 weight without magazine	3.100 kg
M 16 A1 with magazine	3.180 kg
Weight of empty 20-round magazine	0.085 kg
Weight of loaded 20-round magazine	0.320 kg
Weight of empty 30-round magazine	0.110 kg
Weight of loaded 30-round magazine	0.450 kg
Weight of strap	0.182 kg
M 16 weight with loaded 20 round magazine	3.420 kg
M 16 A1 weight with loaded 20 round magazine	3.500 kg
M 16 weight with loaded 30 round magazine	3.550 kg
M 16 A1 weight with loaded 30 round magazine	3.630 kg
Starting weight	2.3 - 3.8 kg
Rate of fire	700 - 950 rounds/minute
Rate of fire - automatic	150/200 rounds/minute
Rate of fire - single shot	45/65 rounds/minute
Ititial velocity	972 meters/second
Initial energy	171 kgm

Make the weapon secure. Using the tip of a bullet, turn the forward pivot which holds the breech casing to the frame. Tip the barrel downwards.

Move the cocking lever forward and extract the moving assembly from the breech case.Bring the cocking lever fully backward then tip it to release it from the groove.

To take apart the breech block, press the spring catch with the tip of a bullet, then hold the block towards the front. It can only be removed when the cocking piece is armed.

Remove the recuperating spring.

To take apart the handguard, pull the rear cup which holds it backwards, then pull apart its two constituent shells.

Corporals T. A. Cooks, D. A. Schwerin and J. E. Koats of the 2nd support battalion of the Marine Service Corps cleaning their M 16 A1s during an exercise
Photo U.S. Marine Corps ▼

▲
Taking the M 16 A1 apart.
Document Colt

This left-handed soldier is probably handicapped by the ejection of spent casings which must almost shave his chin. He appears quite relaxed about it. Even his beret is at a less than regulation angle.

Photo U.S. Army

To disassemble the breech block use the point of a cartridge to release the pin holding the firing pin and separate this from the rest.

Remove the maneuvering pin from the moving head. It is now possible to separate the moving head from the breech.

The weapon is now prepared for day-to-day maintenance.

Cleaning should be concentrated on the barrel, the housing for the interlocking lugs and the interior of the breech.

As necessary, clean the interior of the breech case and the frame of any debris which it may have acquired.

Re-assembly

This is simply a matter of reversing the previous instructions and presents no difficulty. Having

Author's opinion of the M 16 A1

The M16 A1 is light, easily handled, well balanced and has a moderate recoil. Automatic fire is possible even holding the weapon in one hand.

It disassembles easily but maintenance demands care and time.

We did not test the weapon in adverse conditions (e.g. mud, desert).

Putting the M 16 into service did not stop the USA researching new arms materials. In fact, this had been ongoing and field trials of new weapons and leading-edge technology followed each other, though rather erratically. These trials allowed experiments to be made on a number of systems using different ammunition:
- Brass cased flechettes carried by a plastic sabot. When the shot is fired a ram at the base of the casing makes the firing pin recoil. This

M 16 A1 PIP, *precursor of the M 16 A2.*
Photo Colt

The M 16 A2.
Photo Colt

The M 16

The body of the M 16 A2. The new rear sight and the case deflector can clearly be seen.

Photo Jean-Louis Courtois

▶
Instruction manual for the M 16 A2.
Document
U.S. Marine Corps

causes the bolt to unlock, as the recoil of the moving part occurs by the action of the gas on the empty case. The weight of the flechettes varied between 0.64gm and 1.15gm and they could reach an initial speed of 1400 meters per second.This ammunition was reserved for the SP1W and SFR classes, which have now been abandoned.

- Very small caliber darts (4.32mm), fired in three-round salvos. These were used in the SBR project.
- Conventional weapons with a higher performance than those in use (FRS and LMR programs).

TM 05538C-23&P/2

U.S. MARINE CORPS TECHNICAL MANUAL

ORGANIZATIONAL AND INTERMEDIATE MAINTENANCE
(INCLUDING REPAIR PARTS AND SPECIAL TOOLS LIST)

INTRODUCTION	1-1
ORGANIZATIONAL MAINTENANCE INSTRUCTIONS	2-1
INTERMEDIATE MAINTENANCE INSTRUCTIONS	3-1
MAINTENANCE OF AUXILIARY EQUIPMENT	4-1
REFERENCES	A-1
MAINTENANCE ALLOCATION CHART	B-1
REPAIR PARTS AND SPECIAL TOOLS LIST	C-1
EXPENDABLE SUPPLIES AND MATERIALS LIST	D-1
ILLUSTRATED LIST OF MANUFACTURED ITEMS	E-1
TORQUE LIMITS	F-1
ALPHABETICAL INDEX	INDEX-1

RIFLE, 5.56-MM, M16A2 W/E
NSN 1005-01-128-9936

OCTOBER 1984

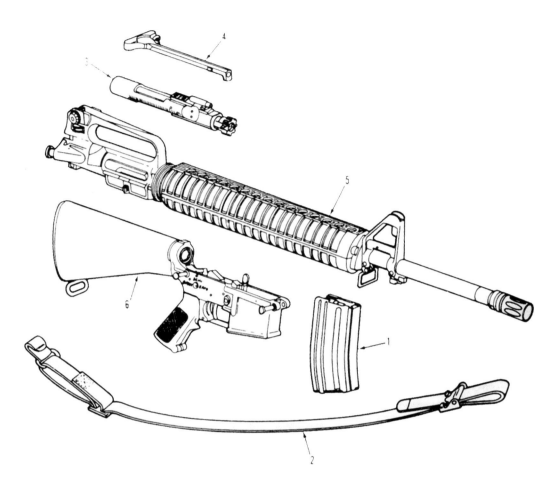

▲

Constituent parts of the M 16 A2:

1 - *Magazine*

2 - *Sling*

3 - *Breech-block assembly*

4 - *Cocking lever*

5 - *Body, barrel, handguard*

6 - *Buttstock, recuperator system and frame assembly*

Document U.S. Marine Corps

• Combustible cartridge cases (ACR and HKG11).

Some of the prototypes developed between 1970 and 1980 were combined with a grenade launcher.

At the same time a study began into the development of a light machine gun firing more effective ammunition than the 5.56mm M 193.

A cartridge was created with a performance midway between that of the .223 and the 7.62mm: this was the 6mm SAW of which there are still two versions: 6 x 45 with a steel or brass case or 6 x 50 in aluminum.

These bullets were tested between 1972 and 1976 and showed sterling qualities but the introduction of a new caliber as the mainstay of the US forces (and consequently of their allies) would no doubt have created serious problems and so it was decided to go back to the 5.56mm ammunition with upgraded performance.

◄

Sighting practice with the M 16 A2.

Photo U.S. Marine Corps

The M 16

Then came the US XM777 cartridge (ball) and the XM778 (tracer) which were rated more highly, as well as Belgian cartridges brought out by F.N. at the same time as the Minimi (M249) machine gun, which was retained for the final phase of the SAW program.

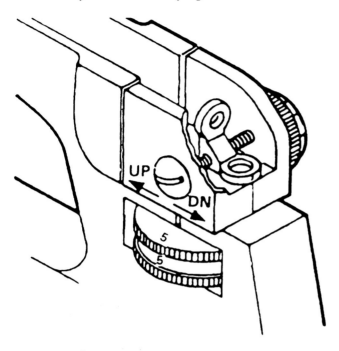

The rear sight of the M 16 A2
Document U.S. Marine Corps

Fabrique Nationale Herstal S.A. created a new family of 5.56mm ammunition for this weapon. These outperformed their US counterparts, but for maximum effect they had to be fired from guns with 180mm (7-inch) rifling.

This new range consisted of a common bullet (SS109), an armor-piercing bullet (P112) and a tracer projectile (L110), which were easily identifiable by their shape which tapered more than those from the US.

Something else had happened during the preceding years. There was a comparative evaluation by NATO of weapons individually and collectively put into service during the 1980s by member countries.

This process, which lasted for two years, allowed them to evaluate the need to provide a second caliber for infantry weapons. The

Belgian 5.56mm with the SS190 bullet was chosen as the base norm.

What became of the M 16 in all this? It is time to say that since it had gone into service those who loved it and those who hated it had continued to tear each other apart. There were countless reports from US politicians on the subject and even more from the Army and the Marines - to say nothing of press releases from the makers!

The most common complaints about the M 16 were:

- its practical range was only 400 meters,
- deficiencies in the sights,
- the low endurance of some of its components,
- problems associated with fouling.

The M 16 in use in the field; here in Saudi Arabia during the First Gulf War.

Photo U.S. Marine Corps

The most severe criticisms came from the US Marines who did not hesitate to draw up a report on individual combat weapons where they envisaged four possibilities:

- to keep the M 16 A1 as it was,
- to improve the weapon, so as to overcome the problems,
- to put the M 14 back into service,
- to adopt a new rifle, even though that would mean a lack of standardization between the arms of the US Marines and the Army.

The second of these solutions was adopted and the J.S.S.A.P. (Joint Service Small Arms Program), the coordinating body, decided to go ahead with production of an improved M 16.

It was named the M 16 A1 PIP, afterwards M 16 A1 E1, and was presented to a commission consisting of Lieutenant Colonel C. J. Pyle, Lieutenant Colonel T. W. Kelly, Major M. W. Smith and Captain R. L. Simmons.

Ballistic trials ran from May to September 1981 at the Aberdeen Proving Ground in Maryland and a second field trial, for military evaluation, took place from October to December.

Completed in 1982, the new weapon was adopted on November 20, 1983 under the name M 16 A2 and was immediately put into service with the Marine Corps. The Army, which had several million M 16 A1s in stock, did not begin to acquire it until 1986.

A comparison between the M 16 A1 and the M 16 A2 shows the following differences:
- buttstock reinforced and lengthened by 16mm. The profile was re-designed, the butt end was wider but still had a housing for anti-fouling equipment, though the shape was different and it was ribbed all over,
- nylon pistol grip with finger rest
- frame fitted with a casing deflector in the form of an extrusion behind the ejection port; thanks to this, ejection to the right was no longer a problem for left-handed firers,
- the shape of the safety on the access plate was redesigned,
- new handguard formed by two symmetrical shells assembled horizontally. The assembly cup was easier to maneuver,
- wider barrel (19.3mm in diameter instead of 14.8mm) with 7-inch rifling for the SS 109 cartridge (the M 193 could no longer be used),
- "full auto" selector replaced by a three-shot automatic fire control limiter,
- sighting and eyepiece made more functional: they were set for firing up to 700 meters and

A Para of the 101st Airborne prepares his M 16 A2 before the Iraq offensive (First Gulf War).
Photo U.S. Army

carried a micrometric height and direction regulator,
- cylindrical cross-sight replaced by a square one,
- a slightly less clumsy muzzle brake made more effective by redesigning the openings.

Thus the M 16 continued. Its manufacture was entrusted to Colt and to the US subsidiary operation of Fabrique Nationale, F.N. Inc. of

During the First Gulf War some M 16 A2s were equipped with a telescopic sight.
Photo U.S. Marine Corps

Maryland. It morphed on into several versions which are described in the following chapters.

Preparation, operation, disassembly and reassembly

Identical to the M 16 A1.

The three-shot automatic selector is an unusual idea. If the first shot has been fired it is possible, if the lever is pressed, to fire two more, but not three. If two shots have been fired, pressing the lever fires only one more shot.

The pressure on the tail of the lever varies for each shot:
- 2.2kgf for the first shot,
- 3.6kgf for the second shot,
- 4.9kgf for the third shot

With his M 16 A2 coupled with a low-light camera, this US soldier wearing a bullet-proof vest, and in constant radio communication with his command line is already a 21st century fighter.
Photo U.S. Army

Long-barreled Derivatives of the M 16

Colt's acquisition of the production license for the AR 15 resulted, as we have seen, in the adoption of the M 16, M16 A1 and later the M 16 A2. To support these weapons, they also had to produce a complete weapons system including:
- long-barreled guns with fixed or telescopic sights,
- short-barreled weapons,
- rifle grenade launchers,
- precision rifles,
- 9mm machine pistols
- section weapons

This weapons system had been revised several times and had opened the way for other models. Thus, among those with long barrels, we find:

Before the M 16 became popular with sportsmen it had already trained millions of combatants as here at Vinh Long camp in 1970
Photo U.S. Army

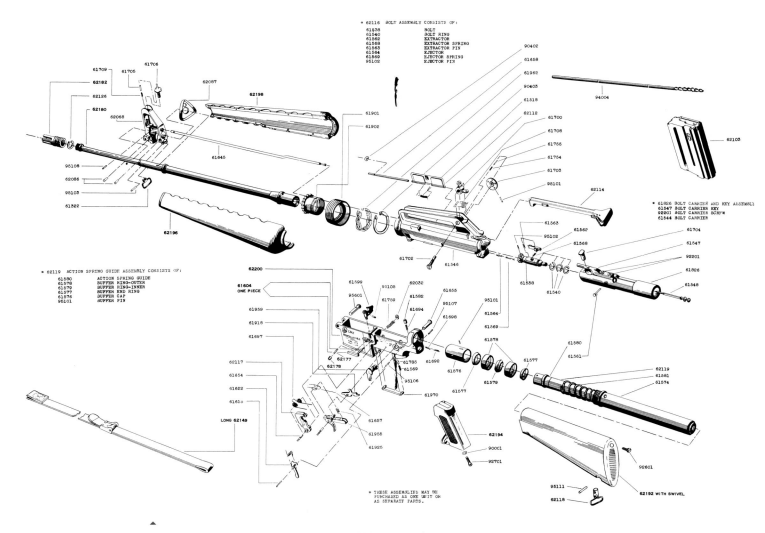

DESCRIPTION OF CONSTITUENT PARTS OF THE AR-15

61546 - Breech casing

62112 - Ejection port shutter

61658 - Shutter spindle

90402 - Shutter spindle stop

61558 - Shutter spring

61700 - Rear sight

61708 - Blade spring

61702 - Drift regulator screw for rear sight

61703 - Regulating disc

61755 - Disc bead stop

95101 - Stop pin for regulator disc

61754 - Bead stop spring

62180 - Barrel

61902 - Nut

61962 - Cup spring

90403 - Circlips

61645 - Adductor tube

95108 - Adductor tube holding pin

62087 - Forward fixing cup of hand guard

62068 - Cross-sight gate

62086 - Cross-sight gate pins (2)

62196 - Left shell of hand guard

62198 - Right shell of hand guard

61706 - Cross sight

61705 - Cross-sight stopper bead

61709 - Stopper bead spring

61322 - Forward sling swivel

95103 - Sling ring pin

62182 - Flash suppressor

62186 - Flash suppressor Grover washer

62114 - Cocking lever

61547 - Adductor tube and bolt junction peg

92201 - Allen key for setting the above

61538 - Bolt head

61540 - Bolt head washers

61562 - Extractor

61568 - Extractor spring

61563 - Extractor pin

61564 - Ejector

61569 - Ejector spring

95102 - Ejector pin

61704 - Bolt head retaining stud

61548 - Percussor

61561 - Percussor retaining pin

61574 - Breech casing extension

95107 - Extension tube retaining pin

61970 - Trigger guard lower arm

95106 - Trigger guard spindle

61604 - Magazine clasp

61759 - Magazine clasp spring

62032 - Magazine clasp button
61599 - Magazine catch
62178 - Catch button
62177 - Catch spring
95105 - Catch pin
61955 - Trigger
61657 - Trigger spring
61654 - Spindle for both trigger and hammer
61918 - Separator
61925 - Separator spring
62117 - Hammer
61697 - Hammer spring
61622 - Automatic fire catch
61615 - Automatic fire catch pin
61582 - Shock absorber stop
61694 - Shock absorber stop pin
61655 - Dismantling peg
61698 - Dismantling peg stopper bead
61692 - Stopper bead spring
62192 - Buttstock
92601 - Butt plate screw
62118 - Rear sling swivel

95111 - Sling ring pin
62119 - Shock absorber / recuperator assembly
61580 - Body of shock absorber
61578 - Shock absorber guidance rings (2)
61579 - Shock absorber guidance ring (1)
61577 - End washer
61576 - Shock absorber ferrule
61581 - Recuperator spring
61559 - Selector
61785 - Selector stop bead
61569 - Stop bead spring
62194 - Pistol grip
92701 - Pistol grip fixing screw
90001 - Fan-shaped washer
95601 - Forward body / breech-case junction peg
62103 - 20-round magazine
94004 - Cleaning rod
91206 - Barrel cleaner
62149 - Sling

Colt Document

Hunters and sport shooters looking to temper recoil need look no further than Colt's new Compensated Match Target Rifles. The 8-round semi-automatic only rifles are available with factory installed upper receiver and barrel assemblies. The MT6700 Flattop receiver allows for scope mounting. Optional sights are available through Colt Optical.

Compensated Match Target Rifle caliber chamberings include .223 HBAR or 7.62x39mm.

FEATURES:
• Improved accuracy
• Suppressed recoil
• Accepts optics
• Ideal for competition

The Colt AR-15 A2 HBAR in the MT 6700 version.
It has a heavy 0.51 meter barrel with 9-inch rifling and has a recoil reducer.
The frame consists of a notched top plate which allows it to use either a traditional handle sight or an optical sight.
Photo Colt.

AR-15 Sporter

In response to the demands of US marksmen Colt offered a semi-automatic version of the M 16. This lacked the button-assisted lock found on the M 16 A1 but it benefited from all the improvements made to the military version. It

1980, production for the civilian market rose to 100,000.

From 1978 there was an AR-15 Sporter carbine, which had a 406mm barrel and the same sliding stock as the machine pistol versions of the M 16 which are described in the next chapter.

Semi-automatic AR-15 Sporter.
Photo Colt

was characterized by its lack of a sear and of anywhere on the frame to put one, so it could not be adapted for military use.

The AR-15 Sporter was usually supplied with a five-shot magazine which is simply a twenty-shot magazine fitted with a capacity-limiting block. 20 and 30 shot magazines could also be used.

This weapon was also used by some police forces in the US and also by UK overseas troops.

The commercial production of the civilian version of the AR-15 began in 1963. Initially, deliveries were sporadic, due to strong military

The left face of the AR-15 Sporter carries the maker's name and the serial number preceded by the letters SP.
Photo Jean Huon

After the appearance of the M 16 A2, the AR-15 altered and was henceforward called the AR-15 A2. It had a reinforced mount like the M 16 A1 and M 16 A2, and the M 16 A2 frame with power-assisted locking and the cartridge case deflector.

Between the end of production of the AR-15 and the completion of the AR-15 A2, Colt produced an improbable selection of hybrid models combining the mounts of the first (AR-15/M 16) and second (M 16 A1/A2) types with the frames of the first (AR-15/M 16), second (M 16 A1) and third (M 16 A2) types!

Three-quarter view of the AR-15 frame. The smooth feed tube with no reinforcing ribs round the magazine holding button can be seen.

Photo Jean Huon

demand but with the return of veterans, orders increased and, from the start of the 1970s up to

Following on from the basic model, categorized as R6000, the civilian versions declined into a multitude of models (more than forty!) which are cataloged in the table following page 107.

The author firing a Colt AR-15 A2 HBAR (Fort Bliss, El Paso, Texas, October 2001).

The sight components have been improved by returning to the basic model. The action is easy and there is little recoil.

The weapon is precise, but no more so than a good 7.62 NATO rifle.

Every movement of the breech allows the vibration of the recuperator spring in the buttstock to be felt. This does have the advantage of warning the user that the last cartridge has been fired.

Photo Colin Doane

Match Target Rifles

In its most recent configurations the semi-automatic carbine developed from the M 16 appeared in the following versions:
- MT 6530, caliber .223 Remington, normal 0.406 meter barrel with 7-inch pitch.
- MT 6551, caliber .223 Remington, normal 0.508 meter barrel with 7-inch pitch.
- MT 6601, caliber .223 Remington, heavy 0.508 meter barrel with 7-inch pitch.
- MT 6700, caliber .223 Remington, heavy 0.508 meter barrel with 9-inch pitch.
- MT 6731, caliber .223 Remington, heavy 0.406 meter barrel with 9-inch pitch.
- MT 6900 DC, caliber .223 Remington, HBAR conversion with heavy barrel.

- MT 6700 DC, caliber .223 Remington with flat-topped frame.
- MT 6850 DC, conversion to 7.62x39 with 0.508 meter barrel.
- MT 6851 DC, conversion to 7.62x39 with 0.508 meter barrel.

M 16

Described in Chapter 3.

Colt Reference, Model 604.

M 16 A1

Described in Chapter 4.

Colt Reference, Model 603.

M 16 A2

Described in Chapter 5

Colt References:
- Model 701 with single shot and volley selector.
- Model 705 with single shot and three-shot volley selector.
- Model 711 with light barrel and rear sight from the M 16 A1; single shot and three-shot volley selector.

M 16 A3

Variation on the M 16 A2 with modular sights and flat breech casing. A slot made it possible to attach: a carrying handle with mechanical sights, an optical sight, a laser indicator or other device to aid sighting.

The M 16 A3 was fitted with a single shot and volley selector.

M 16 A4

Variation on the M 16 A3 with single shot and three-shot volley selector.

CAR-15 Carbine

Developed by Colt when they began to improve the AR-15, the CAR Carbine retained all the elements of the M 16. The barrel is shorter and the muzzle brake is positioned immediately after the fore-sight. There is no bayonet peg and the weapon does not fire grenades.

Because this weapon was not successful with either the commercial or the military worlds it was abandoned and the manufacturer developed other variations.

Specification	M 16 Carbine
Caliber	5.56mm
Ammunition	.223 Remington
Weapon length	0.843 meters
Barrel length	0.368 meters
Weight	2.72kg

M 16 A1 Carbine

Identical to the above but with button-assisted lock.

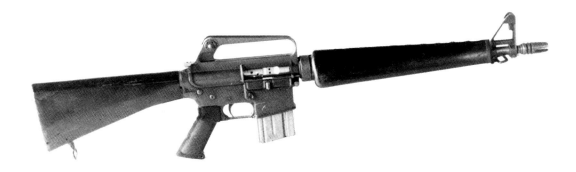

▲
The CAR-15 carbine is an M 16 variant with a 381mm barrel.

Photo Jean Huon

CAR-15 Survival Rifle

Short-barreled weapon with metallic, telescopic stock. The barrel is encased by a cylindrical handguard and ends in a conical flash suppressor. The size of the pistol grip is reduced by half to make the weapon less bulky. The buttstock consists of a tube round which there is a casing with a steel-plated butt end.

M 16 Carbine

The CAR was inconvenient, as it would neither take a bayonet nor fire grenades. Colt therefore created a 368mm-barreled weapon which had a shorter handguard but retained the other elements of the M 16.

AR-15 Sporter Carbine

Semi-automatic commercial version of the AR-15 with 41cm barrel and telescoping stock.

Specifications	AR-15 Carbine
Caliber	5.56mm
Ammunition	.223 Remington
Total length with buttstock extended	0.889 meters
Total length with buttstock retracted	0.806 meters
Barrel length	0.409 meters
Barrel rifling	6 to right
Rifling pitch	178mm
Weight without magazine	2.625kg

M 16 Carbine with telescoping stock

On this model the plastic stock was replaced by the telescoping stock used for the XM 177 machine pistol

CAR-15 survival rifle. It was envisaged that this weapon would be carried dismantled in an airman's pack accompanied by four 20-round magazines.
Graphic Jean Huon

The telescopic stock mounted on the M 16 at the time had been invented by Robert Earl Roy of Colt. It was covered by Patent No. 3.348.328 of October 24th 1967.

A triangular, molded plastic bayonet locking system (US Patent 3.267.601 of 23rd August 1966) was not retained.

M 16 A1 Carbine with telescoping stock

Fitted with a 368mm barrel, button-assisted lock and with telescopic stock.

This model was made by Colt in the US and also in the Philippines.

The M 16 Carbine is a compact version of the M 16 Rifle. It is easier to handle but its effectiveness is not reduced at all.
Photo Colt

XM 177

Previously, US troops had been armed with rifles and machine pistols.

Providing all combatants with assault rifles did not meet with universal approval, some troops finding that the machine pistol was easier to handle than the M 16. To satisfy their demands a short weapon, derived from the M 16, was produced.

It was supplied with a barrel of only 254mm, which terminated in a flash-suppressor. This

was necessary because the flash from firing the shot would have been blinding without it.

The short handguard was identical to that on the carbine. The conventional buttstock was replaced by a metal one containing the shock absorber, the spring box and a retractable moving part. A primitive version of this buttstock had been considered for a survival gun which never went beyond the prototype stage.

This weapon was listed as a machine pistol despite the fact that it did not fire handgun cartridges. Initially known as the CAR-15 Commando, it became the XM 177 and was tested in service by the US Air Force.
Colt Reference: Model 610.

Specifications	XM 177
Caliber	5.56mm
Ammunition	.223 Remington
Total length with buttstock extended	0.787 meters
Total length with buttstock retracted	0.719 meters
Barrel length	0.245 meters
Weight	2.470kg

XM 177 E1

A machine pistol, it had the same characteristics as the preceding model, with the addition of the M 16 button-assisted lock.
Colt Reference: Model 609.

XM 177 E2

Variation on the XM 177 E1 with a 292mm barrel. Used in Vietnam by the Special Forces, it was also known as the Commando Submachine Gun.
Colt Reference: Model 629.

Specifications	XM 177 E2
Caliber	5.56mm
Ammunition	.223 Remington
Total length with buttstock extended	0.830 meters
Total length with buttstock retracted	0.762 meters
Barrel length	2.292 meters
Weight	2.500kg

GAU-5/A/A

US Air Force machine pistol with 9fi-inch (241mm) barrel.
Colt Reference: Model 649.

COLT INDUSTRIES OPERATING CORP
WEAPONS DIVISION

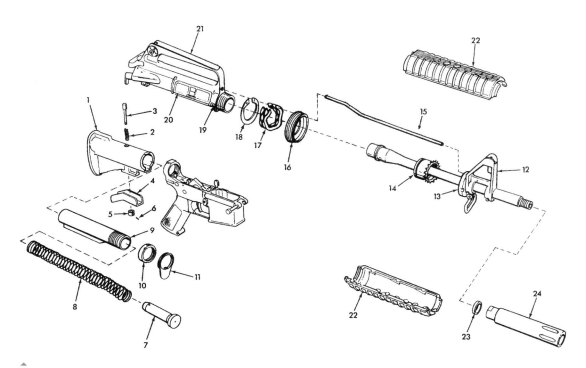

EXPLODED DIAGRAM OF THE XM 177 SERIES WEAPONS

1 - Buttstock
2 - Buttstock lock spring
3 - Buttstock lock pin
4 - Buttstock lock
5 - Washer
6 - Peg
7 - Shock absorber
8 - Recuperator spring
9 - Spring guide tube
10 - Guide tube screw-nut
11 - Tube assembly plate
12 - Sight mounting

13 - Forward seat of handguard
14 - Screw-nut
15 - Adductor tube
16 - Rear seat of handguard
17 - Scraper spring
18 - Circlips
19 - Breech casing
20 - Ejection port shutter
21 - Carrying handle
22 - Handguard (2)
23 - Washer
24 - Flash suppressor

M 16 A1 with telescopic buttstock.
Dessin Jean Huon

GAU-5/A/B

US Air Force version of the XM 177 E1.
Colt Reference: Commando Model 630

GAU-5/P

Model with 368mm barrel, used by the US Air Force.

M 231

The development of a new program of combat vehicles for the US Infantry made clear the need for a weapon which could be fired from inside a vehicle.

A soldier of the 3rd
Battalion of the 1st
Infantry Regiment (11th
Air Assault Division)
cleaning his XM 177
during Operation
Cigar Island
north of Chu Lei,
November 7th 1968.

Photo U.S. Army

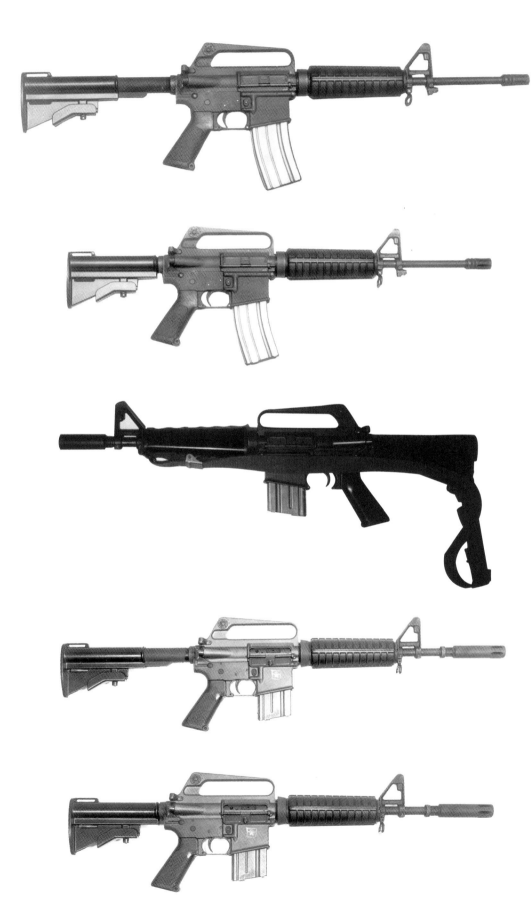

◄
M 16 A1 sub-machine gun.
This 254mm barrel version
is identical to the XM 177
E1 apart from the flash
suppressor.
Photo Colt

◄
The M 16 A1 Carbine with
telescoping buttstock has a
368mm barrel. The total
length of 0.889 meter is
reduced to 812mm when its
buttstock is retracted. It
weighs 2.620kg.
Photo Colt

◄
The Frankford Arsenal's
1987 attempt to shorten the
M 16.

◄
XM 177 E2 'Commando
Sub-machine Gun.' Used by
US Special Forces during the
Vietnam War.
Photo Colt

XM 177 E1 Sub-machine gun used by US ground troops. It has a 10-inch (254mm) barrel with a sliding buttstock made of nylon-sheathed aluminum.

US Army photograph taken at Khe San (B Company 5th Battalion 7th Cavalry Regiment, 1st Cavalry Division (Airmobile).

In 1972 comparative tests were made of a modified M 16 and the HK 53 (from the German manufacturer Heckler & Koch). The HK 53 was quickly rejected and the M 16 continued to be improved until it was finally adopted in January 1980 as the M 231 or the FPW (Firing Port Weapon).

The M 231 had a short barrel, heavier than that of an infantry rifle so as to minimize overheating, which permitted an accelerated firing rate (1100/1200 rounds per minute). To avoid the risk of spontaneous ignition in the barrel, the weapon fired with the breech open and only in volleys. The moving part remained in the rear position between each volley.

The M 231 was swivel-mounted and the sighting was achieved by the vehicle's gunner's sight allowing for the fact that it fired only tracer bullets. To stop empty cartridge cases flying about inside the vehicle they were collected in a bag fixed to the right of the frame. A flexible tube connected this bag to the exterior of the vehicle to allow excess fumes to be dispersed.

The HK 53, unfortunate rival of the M 231.
Photo Heckler & Koch

Specifications	M 231
Caliber	5.56mm
Ammunition	.223 Remington
Total length	0.724 meters
Barrel length	0.368 meters
Weight	4.300kg
Firing rate	1100/1200 per min

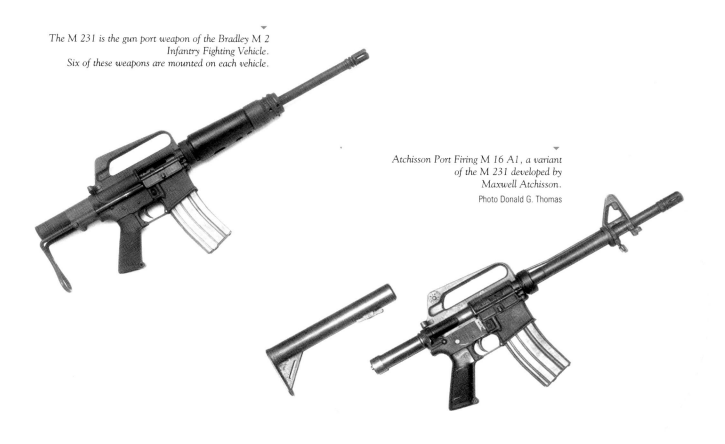

The M 231 is the gun port weapon of the Bradley M 2
Infantry Fighting Vehicle.
Six of these weapons are mounted on each vehicle.

Atchisson Port Firing M 16 A1, a variant
of the M 231 developed by
Maxwell Atchisson.
Photo Donald G. Thomas

The armored infantry transport and escort vehicle
(Infantry Fighting Vehicle) IFV M2 is powerfully
armed. Its two-seater, gyro-stabilized turret carries a
25mm "Chain Gun" M 242 firing either armor-
piercing or incendiary shells, a 7.62mm M 240 and
a double rocket-launching ramp for Improved TOW
missiles.

The combat group can also deploy six swivel-
mounted M 231s, two on each side and two at the
rear port.

The M 2's hull is armored with aluminum alloy, it
is amphibious and suitable for combat in a NBC
warfare zone. It was devised and manufactured by
FMC

Photo Hughes Helicopter

Specifications	Model 723	Model 733
Caliber	5.56mm	5.56mm
Ammunition	5.56mm NATO	5.56mm NATO
Total length with buttstock extended	0.840 meters	0.760 meters
Total length with buttstock retracted	0.760 meters	0.680 meters
Barrel length	0.370 meters	0.290 meters
Barrel rifling	6 to right	6 to right
Rifling pitch	178mm	178mm
Weight without magazine	2.700kg	2.590kg
Weight with magazine loaded	3.150kg	3.040kg
Magazine capacity	30 rounds	30 rounds
Firing rate	750-950 rounds/minute	700-900 rounds/mn
Initial velocity (M 193)	921 meters/second	839 meters/second
Initial velocity (5.56mm NATO)	906 meters/second	795 meters/second
Initial energy (M 193)`	155kg	28kg
Initial energy (5.56mm NATO)	167kg	286kg
Effective range (M 193)	360 meters	300 meters
Effective range (5.56mm NATO)	600 meters	500 meters

In Vietnam the use of carbines was marginal and it was the standard version which was most used.
Photo U.S. Army

Although every infantryman on board the M 2 armored vehicle had his own individual weapon (M 16 or M 203) each could detach the M 231 and use it as a machine pistol. For this purpose a sliding stock made of steel wire and a retractable cross-sight were mounted on the FPW.

M 16 A2 Commando Model 733.
Photo Colt

M 16 A2 Carbine

A weapon with a light 370mm barrel with telescoping stock, single-shot and volley selector. The telescoping stock and the handguard of the weapons arising from the AR-15, M 16 and M 16 A1 were in light alloy. Those mounted on the derivatives of the M 16 A2 were of high-resistance plastic.

An M 203 grenade launcher mounted on an M 6 carbine.
Photo U.S. Army

Colt Reference: Model 723 light-barreled Carbine.

A new version furnished with a barrel allowing for the connection of a 40mm M 203 grenade launcher was designated Colt Model 777 Carbine.

M 16 A2 Commando

M 16 A2 with telescoping stock, short, light barrel and single-shot or volley selector.

Colt Reference: Commando Model 733.

M 4 Carbine

The M 4 was an M 16 A2 with a modular breech casing (like the M 16 A3 and A4), which would take mechanical or optical sights.

It replaced the M 9 pistol, the M 3 A1 submachine gun and the M 16 A2 as the main weapon of certain units (Rangers, Paratroopers, Navy SEALs, Special Forces). It was also delivered to elite units in several other countries.

M 4 Carbine.
Photo Colt

M 6 *Carbine*
Photo Colt

M 6 Carbine

This was an improved M 4 with a short barrel.

It could deploy an M 203 grenade launcher.

M 23 A1 Carbine

This was an M 4 carbine furnished with a telescope connected to an electronic fire control system.

The M 16 is provided with a 22mm diameter flash suppressor, which enables it to launch grenades without any additional accessory.

Finned grenade mounted on the M 16.
Photo Jean Huon

This process places increased strains on the weapon and it is strongly recommended not to support the butt on a hard surface. Previously this type of grenade was widespread in the US Army and it has remained in service in most European countries. However, it fell into disuse in the US, where an anti-personnel grenade launcher was developed, by means of a weapon which resembled a large, single-shot hunting piece, the M 79.

Caliber: 40mm
Total length: 0.758 meter
Barrel length: 0.356 meter
Weight: 2.950kg

Photo Jean Huon

This was equipped with a drop barrel for loading, it was 40mm caliber and it had six rifling grooves. The stock was specially designed to allow effective sighting in good conditions.

The anti-recoil butt plate was made of honeycombed rubber.

Putting such a weapon into service impaired the unity of construction which had previously existed. To remedy this it was decided to

The M 79 has a barrel which tips like that of a shotgun.
Photo Jean Huon

The special trajectory of the 40mm grenade calls for the use of a very sophisticated rear sight.
Photo Jean Huon

produce a 40mm tube as an adaptation to the assault rifle.

The first attempts began with the M 14 and were followed up with the M 16.

XM 148

Invented by Henry A. Into and patented April 21st 1970 as No. 3.507.067, the CGL-4, tested under the name XM 148, was a 40mm barrel for adding to the M 16 A1. This barrel, mounted on a slide and pushed forward for loading, required

40mm Colt XM 148 grenade launcher mounted on the M 16 A1.
Photo U.S. Army

M 203 grenade launcher mounted on the M 16 A1.
Caliber: 40mm
Total length: 0.380 meter
Barrel length: 0.300 meter
Empty weight: 1.360kg
Photo Colt

a maneuvering handle, with a firing key. The first versions had a firing-key system which consisted of a back-curved lever placed below the trigger guard. The XM 148 could be mounted on a variety of assault rifles. The adaptation for the M 16 necessitated the use of a special, honeycombed, cylindrical handguard.

After several years' experience in Vietnam, the US Army finally rejected the XM 148. There were similar conversions by:

- Aero-Jet,
- Colt (CGL-5),
- Philco-Ford.

M 203

Abandoning the XM 148 led to the US Army developing a new 40mm grenade launcher which could be mounted on the M 16 A1.

This barrel, adopted in 1969 as the M 203, was conceived by the AAI Corporation and was manufactured by Colt from January 1971. It was used in varying numbers by the US Army for particular missions by combat groups.

The M 203 consisted of a mount which was fixed under the M 16's barrel.
  • At the rear of this mount is the trigger mechanism, which consists of a percussion block with a firing lever and a trigger guard. The safety catch is placed in front of the trigger and prevents the finger from being inserted in the trigger guard while it is engaged.
  • The barrel slides under the mount for loading, and for ease of maneuver the rear portion has a grooved lining. It is locked by a lever to the left and above the barrel.

The conventional handguard was replaced by a square-section one which had holes in it to facilitate cooling.

The M 203 had two sights: one for direct fire, being a retractable scale placed behind the foot of the cross-sight.

It was marked in 50 meter gradations for firing between 50 and 200 meters; one for high angle fire, formed by a sight bar placed to the left of the carrying handle, with gradations of 25-400 meters.

XM 177 E2 / M 203

This model was the result of an inovation in the field, developed by Sergeant A. G. McCulloch Jr. of 73rd Infantry Division Rangers. He succeeded in mounting an M 203 grenade launcher on an XM177 sub-machine gun.

To do this the handguard had to be modified and the sights of the 40mm barrel also had to be removed. Sighting was done by guess but the weapon remained very effective at short distance.

The JCMI assembly is equally adaptable to most assault rifles.
Photo J.C. Manufacturing Co.

Atchisson Grenade Launcher

Maxwell G. Atchisson was a former US Marine who contributed to the development of a number of automatic weapons and their

The M 16 A2 equipped with the M 203 weighs about 5kg.
The maximum range of the grenade launcher is 400 meters.
Photo Colt

accessories. He is responsible for several adaptations of the M 16 which will be mentioned later in this work.

To enable every combatant to have at his command firepower comparable to that of the the soldier with an M 203, Maxwell Atchisson invented a demountable tube to fit the M 16 without interfering with its ability to fire cartridges.

This tube was made up of a rifled barrel which could be unscrewed for loading and was

Specialized sight components of the M 203.
Photo Colt

attached to a rear spigot when it was mounted. The whole thing was fixed at the muzzle of the weapon by means of a brace supported by the flash suppressor, and by a rear lock which engaged with the bayonet peg. Firing was achieved by pulling the rear ring, thus arming and releasing the firing pin, which was attached to a blade spring. The tube could be carried quite safely when loaded because it had a device to preclude firing when the rear lock was not engaged in the bayonet peg. Though it was patented on 1st January 1974, this device was never adopted by the US Army.

Pvt. 1st Class G. W.
Hancock carrying the M 203
during an exercise.
Photo US Marine Corps

RAW grenade launcher

The 40mm grenade had limited effectiveness in anti-personnel terms and troops found themselves unprovided for when they faced an entrenched enemy or an armored vehicle, and had to rely on those firing LAW M 72 A2 rocket launchers.

The Brunswick Company's Defense Division tried to respond to this problem by developing a launcher which fired a self-propelling missile dubbed the Rifleman Assault Weapon (RAW).

This appliance is made up of a yoke which can be adapted instantly and without modification to either the M 16 or M 16 A1. Mounting the RAW launcher in no way impedes the firing of cartridges and it is in fact the cartridge ball which secures the launch of the missile.

This latter is made up of a sphere containing the explosive charge with a fuse in front which detonates on impact. In the middle is the propulsive charge with its blast pipe. A stabilizing tail projects from the rear of the missile.

Soldier with an M 203 in ambush position behind a tree.
Photo U.S. Marine Corps

Cpl. D. W. Mitchal, Command Battalion of the 8th Marine Regiment, mounts guard during a NATO exercise in Norway in September 1976.
Photo U.S. Marine Corps

When the shot is fired, some of the bullet's propulsion gas penetrates into a channel on the launcher which links the weapon's muzzle brake with the RAW grenade bracket. The projectile's tail is equipped with needle bearings and this gas makes it rotate at high speed and launch slowly. Several meters from the weapon the propellant charge goes into action, ensuring the high-speed continuation of the trajectory while the rotation is maintained.

The practical range of the RAW is greater than 200 meters in direct fire and the makers envisaged improving this until it reached 2000 meters. The assembled RAW weighs 2.7kg and the charge is made up of 1359gm of explosive, which allows it to pierce 20cm of reinforced concrete.

Another M 203 in action, this time during the 'Kangaroo III' combined maneuvers in Australia with US, Australian and New Zealand troops October 25th 1979.

Photo U.S. Army.

Non-regulation mounting of an M 203 on an XM 177 E2.
It is an extremely light weapon which measures about 85cm.

Photo A. G. Mc Culloch Jr.

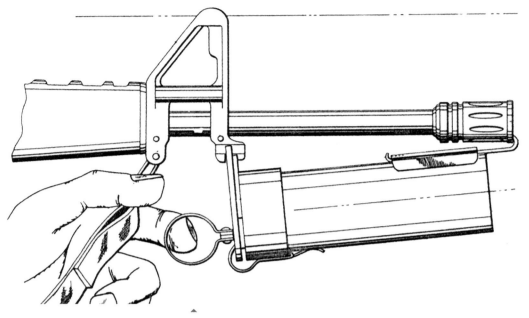

The Atchisson grenade-launching tube mounted on the M 16.
Document attached to the patent

The RAW is effective against vehicles and light armor, or against an enemy entrenched in buildings or light casemates. This type of weapon was revealed in 1980 and was tested by the Advanced System Concept Office.

The 40mm grenade is composed of an aluminum shell with two compartments (chamber above, pressure below), which allows a heavy projectile to be launched without causing too great a recoil.

The projectile consists of a fragmentation sphere topped by an aluminum nose which overlaps the fuse. Its initial speed is 75 meters/second and the fragments of the grenade are lethal within a radius of 5 meters.

The safety distance for an unprotected user is 30 meters.

There is a vast number of projectiles for 40mm weapons; those most commonly used by the military are:

M 406	explosive
M 443	explosive armor-piercing
M 567	anti-personnel
M 407	practice/training
M 787	practice/training

Photo Jean Huon

MECAR adaptation

To satisfy the need for troops using the M 16 who wanted to be able to fire 22mm finned grenades, the Belgian company MECAR S.A. suggested installing a clip at the end of the M 16's barrel which allowed finned grenades to be fired in all positions. it could be installed by simply removing the flash suppressor.

Firing a MECAR grenade rifle armed with a bullet trap, with an M 16.
Photo MECAR

M 16 A2/M 203

The M 203 went on giving great satisfaction and was generally supplied with the M 16 A2 in its normal version or as the M 6 Carbine.

The M 203 was also made under license by Diemaco of Canada.

MECAR S.A. specialized in the production of rifle grenades. It had produced a wide range of devices which could be propelled by a ball cartridge because a Bullet Trap Unit held the missile level with the fin.

J.C. Manufacturing

J.C. Manufacturing of Spring Lake Minnesota offered an improved version of the M 203. It comprised an ultra-rapid assembly device to be used with the Armson OEG sight.

This model was not adopted.

M 16 fitted with RAW grenade launcher. The 140mm diameter projectile works by deferred ignition and can blow a 35mm diameter hole in a concrete wall 20cm thick.
Photo Brunswick Defense.

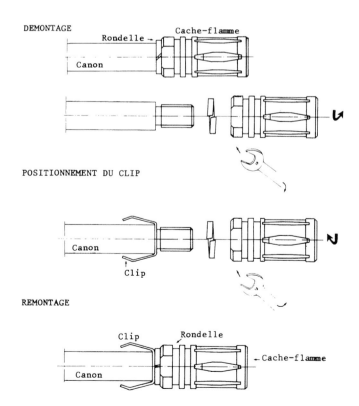

Retaining clip for 22mm finned grenade.
Document MECAR

Design for the Colt CMG-2 machine gun.
Photo Colt

Colt HBAR

The arms system invented by Armalite had already foreseen the need for a belt-fed light machine gun developed from the AR-10. A weapon of similar type had been developed by Colt at the start of the AR-15 program. This was rapidly abandoned and gave way to a new idea - that of a 5.56mm machine gun.

This did not stop the Hartford firm from offering a machine version of its assault gun, adapted from the beginning to the M 16, the M 16 A1 and now the M 16 A2.

Designated the HBAR (Heavy Barrel Assault Rifle), this model was presented as an assault weapon with selective fire, equipped with a heavier barrel which allowed it to sustain a higher practical rate of fire. A folding stand with two telescoping legs was fixed to the end of the barrel.

The XM 106 is an M 16 A1 given the role of a submachine gun. It was not retained by the SAW program.
Photo U.S. Army

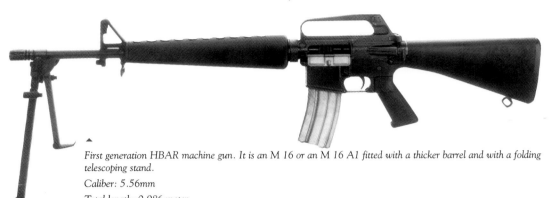

First generation HBAR machine gun. It is an M 16 or an M 16 A1 fitted with a thicker barrel and with a folding telescoping stand.

Caliber: 5.56mm

Total length: 0.986 meter

Barrel length: 0.50 meter

Weight without magazine: 4.580kg

Photo Colt

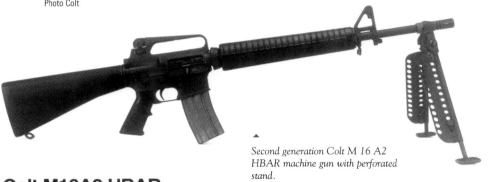

Second generation Colt M 16 A2 HBAR machine gun with perforated stand.

Colt Model 741

Photo Colt

Colt M16A2 HBAR—Model 741

Colt also offered another weapon, more fitted to the role of the light machine gun. It has a heavy barrel, a perforated, square-section handguard, a forward grip and a stand with cooling fins.

The weapon fires with an open breech and because of this does not have button closure.

The rate of fire is between 600 and 800 rounds/minute.

The variant can be adapted to either the M 16 A1 (above) or the M 16 A2 (below).

Photo Colt

XM 106

The XM 106 was an experimental weapon developed at the request of the US Marines within the framework of the SAW (Squad Automatic Weapons) program.

The XM 106 was a heavy-barreled weapon with central fork support. The barrel was interchangeable, the hand guard came apart in situ, the forward portion remaining attached to the barrel, and it had a pistol grip which gave ease of grasp and manipulation.

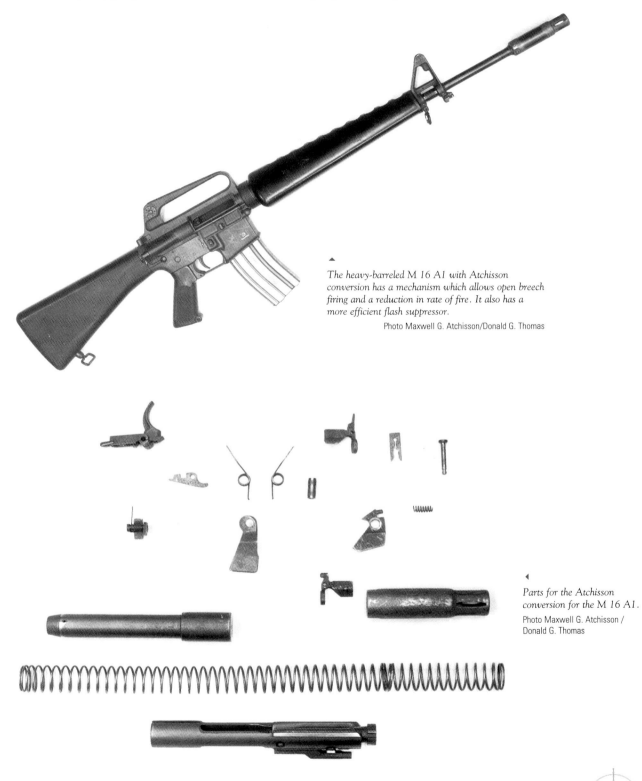

The heavy-barreled M 16 A1 with Atchisson conversion has a mechanism which allows open breech firing and a reduction in rate of fire. It also has a more efficient flash suppressor.

Photo Maxwell G. Atchisson/Donald G. Thomas

Parts for the Atchisson conversion for the M 16 A1.
Photo Maxwell G. Atchisson /
Donald G. Thomas

The M 16

The machine-gun modifications of the M 16 were tested against other automatic weapon groups of the same caliber, among which were the following:
- HK 23 A1, a German weapon (XM 262)
- XM 248 from Ford Aerospace,

- Minimi from Fabrique Nationale (M 249). This was the weapon that was chosen on September 19th 1980 for the final phase of the SAW program. Following the conclusion of the program it has been adopted by most NATO countries.

Atchisson M 16 A1 machine gun with stand and Tri-Mag.
Caliber: 5.56mm
Total length: 1.004 meter
Barrel length: 0.508 meter
Weight without magazine: 4.350kg
Rate of fire: 300-400 rounds/minute
Magazine capacity: 3x30 rounds

Photo Maxwell G. Atchisson/Donald G. Thomas

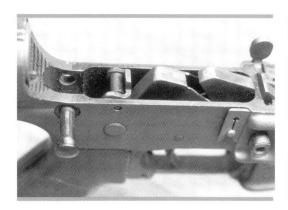

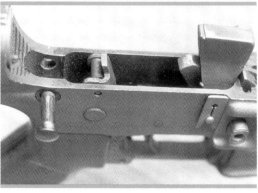

Firing mechanism for Atchisson conversion with hammer cocked.
Photo Maxwell G. Atchisson/Donald G. Thomas

Firing mechanism for the Atchisson conversion with hammer released.
Photo Maxwell G. Atchisson/Donald G. Thomas

For more than 15 years a replacement for the M 60 machine gun (above) based on the M 16 was sought without success.
Author's Collection

SAW program prototype XM 248.
Photo U.S. Army

M 16 A1 Atchisson Machine Gun

During the 1970s a large number of arms manufacturers, Vietnam veterans and researchers of all kinds suggested many improvements and modifications to the M 16 A1. One of the most prolific of these was, without a doubt, Maxwell Atchisson and we shall consider some of his ideas. He came up with a device to enable the M 16 A1 to be used as a machine gun by replacing several elements.

The efficiency of automatic fire was increased by reducing the rate of fire to 300-400 rounds per minute. Further, the Atchisson conversion only worked with the breech open, allowing improved cooling of the barrel and eliminating the risk of premature firing in an overheated tube. The recoil of the M 16 A1 with this modification was lessened and accuracy of fire was increased.

The conversion could be used on any M 16 A1 by simply changing parts without modifying the weapon itself. It consisted of:

- a new trigger system with spring catch, automatic cocking piece and retainer,
- a different shock absorber,
- a return spring with more rigidity,
- a modified breech block,
- a more effective flash suppressor.

Before the adoption of the M 249, new light machine gun ammunition had been considered.

From right to left: 5.56 x 45; experimental cartridges 6 x 45 SAW, 6 x 50 SAW.

This collection of devices could be mounted on the standard M 16 A1 or, more especially, on the heavy barrel version. In the latter case it was possible to add the Tri Mag feed system described later.

Ultimately the MINIMI range made by Fabrique Nationale was selected as the infantry machine gun. It was known as the M 249.

Photo F.N.

Colt optical sight mounted on an AR-15.

Sharpshooter rifle developed by Colt.

This model remained as a prototype. It became the XM 16 E1 No. 575627.

Photo Colt

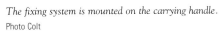

The fixing system is mounted on the carrying handle.

Photo Colt

US Army marksmen had for a long time been equipped with weapons firing NATO 7.62mm cartridges:

- M 21, a semi-automatic rifle derived from the National Match M 14 for the US Army, fitted with a variable 3x to 9x Leatherwood sight.
- M 24, Remington 700 repeating carbine for the US Marines. This was derived from a hunting rifle and had a Redfield 3x to 9x sight.

Star Tron MK 303A mounted on an M 16 rifle. This is a light-amplifying night sight.

Length of appliance: 33cm

Weight: 2320gm

Magnification: 6.8x

Photo Smith & Wesson

The M 16

Colt Telescope

The Colt company offered a very compact optical sight with 3x magnification. It was mounted on the carrying handle by a removable socket.

This sight was employed mainly by sharpshooters and hunters using the AR-15 Sporter

M 16 A1 Sniper

Colt had also manufactured a prototype sniper's weapon derived from the M 16. A high-magnification sight was mounted on a machined rail in a base, which replaced the carrying handle. A silencer could be fitted at the end of the barrel.

▲
The NVS 520 was sold by the Standard Equipment Company of Milwaukee, Wisconsin.
Photo SECO

▲
A night vision Starlight mounted on the M 16 A1 of Michael Largo of the 9th Infantry Division during 'Operation Bearcat' in Vietnam, October 23, 1967.
Photo U.S. Army

The M 1600 is a precision weapon developed by Accuracy Systems Inc. of Tempe, Arizona. It consists of the frame of an M 16 A1 on which is mounted a heavy barrel with a muzzle brake. The perforated tube forming the handguard is not in contact with the barrel. The ant-kick pad and the ergonomic pistol grip make for more comfortable firing. The weapon can accommodate a firing telescope or any other aid to sighting.

Graphic Jean Huon

Star Tron

The Star Tron was a night-fighting device using light amplification. There were two models, the MK 202 A and the MK 203 A, which could be used to observe a man at 400-800 meters using ambient light.

This device could be used on its own or in combination with a firing sight, in which case it could be adapted to a number of different weapons.

The Star Tron was marketed by the Police and Security Division of Smith & Wesson.

Starlight

The Starlight was an earlier light-amplifying night sight than the Star Tron and was used in Vietnam.

N V S 520

The Ni-Tec Vision Systems was also a light-amplifying night sight, which comprised a 95mm or 115mm scope with catadioptric lenses, for observation or firing in the dark.

Laser sights

Hydra Systems International of Bridgeport, Connecticut offered a laser sight mechanism, which was fixed under the stock of the M 16. It consisted of a cylindrical fixture projecting a light ray which showed up as a red circle marking the point of impact.

An identical mechanism was developed by the Laser Products Corporation of Fountain Valley, California. It was placed above the handguard

AR-15 equipped with a laser sight.
This adds about 1kg to the weight.
Photo Laser Products Corp.

and required modification of both the carrying handle and the sight before it could be fitted.

The M 16

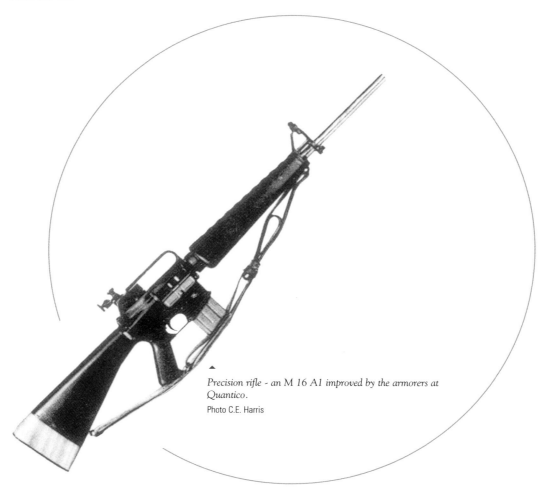

Precision rifle - an M 16 A1 improved by the armorers at Quantico.
Photo C.E. Harris

M 16 for competition shooting

Americans are skillful enthusiasts for long-distance precision shooting. Competitive events at 300 and 600 yards are particularly popular and at these distances weapons firing .30-06 or 7.62mm NATO ammunition are perfectly acceptable.

This is not the case with 5.56mm cartridges. In this case the marksmen use specially loaded cartridges firing heavier bullets, as well as M 16's adapted for enhanced performance.

Both military and civilian arms companies produced similar applications, to satisfy the weapons regulations of the NRA and the NBPRP.

The most recent innovations have involved the installation of a micrometric calibrated sighting loop above the carrying handle which has been milled, and also the fitting of a new barrel.

There have been other improvements to the stock and the handguard.

M 16 A1 National Match developed by the US Army at Rock Island Arsenal.
Photo C.E. Harris

Some examples:

- M 16 A1 conversion by US Marine Corps armorers at Quantico Base, Virginia in 1972. The buttstock was lengthened with a wooden shoe and micrometric adjustment sights were installed. The original barrel was replaced by one which was thicker and made of stainless steel, measuring 0.61 meters with 12-inch rifling in the bore.
- M 16 A1 adapted by the US Navy, with a heavy barrel and 9-inch rifling.
- M 16 A1 National Match, developed experimentally by the US Army at the Rock Island Arsenal. It had a Redfield International sight and a heavy 24-inch barrel. The buttstock had a rubber shoe and the handguard was replaced by a 44mm diameter steel tube which did not touch the barrel and allowed it to vibrate freely.
- M 16 A1 Match, built by the Rodman Laboratory with a normal length Hart barrel with 9-inch rifling. The carrying handle was omitted, which made it possible to lower the aiming line. The sight was placed on a housing at the extremity of the barrel, which could vibrate freely as it was not in contact with the tubular handguard.

Colt match rifles

- Match version of the AR-15/M 16 A1 with adjustable cheek rest.
- Colt Accurized Rifle: frame without handgrip like the M 16 A3, with optical sight, cylindrical handguard, heavy 61cm barrel without sight holder and with 228mm rifling; the caliber was .223 and it had a 9-round magazine. Colt Reference CR 6724.

Improved M 16 A1 with buttstock extension and precision sight.
Photo C.E. Harris

*Precision rifle prototype based on the M 16
made by Rodman Laboratories.*

Photo C.E. Harris

- Match Target HBAR: frame without handgrip with optical sight, conventional handguard, 51cm heavy bare-muzzled barrel (flash-suppressor attachable), 178mm rifling; caliber .223 or 7.62x39, 9-round magazine. Colt Reference MT 6601.
- Match Target Competition HBAR: frame without handgrip, taking an optical sight, conventional handguard, 51cm heavy bare-muzzle barrel (flash-suppressor attachable), 228mm rifling; caliber .223 or 7.62x39, 9-round Colt Reference MT6700.
- Match Target Competition HBAR II; frame without hand grip, optical sight, conventional handguard, bare-muzzle heavy 40cm barrel (flash-suppressor attachable), 228mm rifling; caliber .223, 9-round magaznine. Colt Reference MT6731.

Customizations

If the 1970s and 1980s were the golden age of inventors of military adaptations to the M 16 A1, the 1990s were the years when arms manufacturers offered a multitude of variations designed to make the M 16 a high-precision weapon for long-distance shooting.

Most of the models drew their inspiration from the M 16 A3, with a flat breech casing capable of taking a multitude of accessories.

Still More . . .

There are numerous copies and derivatives of the M 16, which are described in detail in Chapter 15.

The M 16 as a sub-machine gun

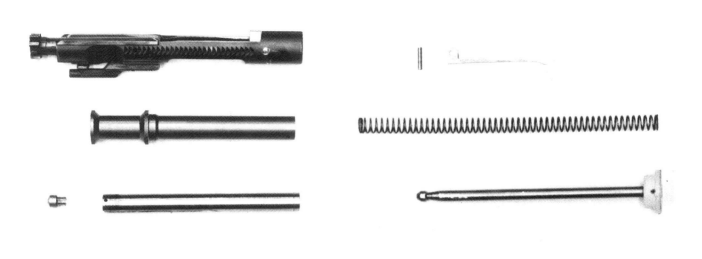

Some elements of the Atchisson conversion for the 9mm machine pistol derived from the M 16 A1.

Photo Maxwell G. Atchisson / Donald G. Thomas

We have seen that there were telescopic-sight and short-barreled versions of the M 16. These weapons were sometimes referred to as machine pistols, which was not an entirely accurate description because they used assault rifle cartridges. Nevertheless there were weapons, derived from the M 16 A1, which could claim to be true machine pistols because they fired 9mm Parabellum bullets.

The first were produced by Maxwell Atchisson who gave them the same trigger system as on the machine gun described above. The weapon had an unlocked breech, whose firing cup and extractor had been modified.

The shock absorber had also been subjected to alterations while a smaller recuperator spring with a guide pin had been fitted. It was equipped with a new barrel and the gas cylinder was omitted.

Atchisson machine pistol derived from the XM 177 E2.

Ammunition: 9mm Parabellum

Total length: 0.695 meter

Length with buttstock retracted: 0.609 meter

Barrel length: 0.260 meter

Weight: 2.260kg

Magazine capacity: 25 rounds

Photo Maxwell G. Atchisson / Donald G. Thomas

▲

Atchisson machine pistol with perforated cooler tube.

Ammunition: 9mm Parabellum

Total length: 0.695 meter

Length with buttstock retracted: 0.609 meter

Barrel length: 0.260 meter

Weight: 2.150kg

Magazine capacity: 25 rounds

Photo Maxwell G. Atchisson/Donald G. Thomas

Some time later, Colt took up the idea and from then on produced a range of machine pistols made on the model of the M 16 and its derivatives.

Colt machine pistols

Towards the end of 1985 Colt began the commercial production of a machine pistol which fired a 9mm Parabellum bullet.

The weapon worked with a closed breech and had a telescopic sight. The sight was composed of an aperture on a tipping bracket, giving a range of 50-100 meters. It used the same magazine as the UZI machine pistol.

Quite recently Colt has developed the MP 24 AR, a carbine with fixed buttstock, constructed on the foundation of the M 16 A2 and firing .45 ACP cartridges.

Atchisson semi-automatic carbine. This weapon operates with closed breech and fires only single shots. The barrel is lengthened by a noise suppressor invented by Military Arms Corporation.

Ammunition: 9mm Parabellum

Total length: 0.838 meter

Length with buttstock retracted: 0.752 meter

Barrel length: 0.406 meter

Weight: 2.950kg

Magazine capacity: 25 rounds

Photo Maxwell G. Atchisson/Donald G. Thomas

Colt machine pistol.
Photo Colt

The Colt machine pistol is used by specialist units of the City of Atlanta Police.
Photo IDC

Magazines

Initially the M 16 was supplied with a crimped-wall magazine like that on the AR-10, made of aluminum, and it had a 20-round capacity.

20-round magazine for the M 16. It weighs 86gm empty and 320gm loaded.

In the 30-round magazine these figures are 110gm and 450gm respectively.

Photo Jean Huon

With the first contract with the US Air Force (1963-1968), a ribbed magazine with aluminum elevator took its place.

Then came the 'Vietnam' model with the base and elevator in black plastic. These were produced by Colt Adventureline or Simmonds.

In use it became clear that this magazine's capacity was inadequate and it was replaced by a curved, 30-round magazine at the time that the M 16 went into service.

This magazine was made in the same way as the 20-round one. The early magazines had a green plastic elevator, later changed to black. They were produced in the millions and there are still some ten firms making them today.

The most recent examples have a Teflon-coated lining.

These two magazines can be loaded with loose cartridges or, using an accessory, a clip of ten cartridges to make reloading easier.

One of those principally responsible for the development of Colt's M 16 magazines was Robert D. Fremont. He was responsible for the following versions:
- the curved 30-round magazine (US Patent No. 3.440.751 of April 29, 1969);
- a plastic magazine with detachable cover and removable elevator pin for ease of loading (US Patent No. 3.453.762 of July 8, 1969);
- a modification of the magazine lips to avoid double feeding (US Patent No. 3.619.929 of November 16, 1971).

In addition to the 20- or 30-round aluminum regulation US Army magazines, there were also commercially available magazines also made of aluminum, steel plate, either bronzed or Teflon-coated, which would take 5, 8, 10, 20, 30, 40, 50 or 55 rounds.

These curved magazines were sold by various mail order companies, particularly by

Markings on the first magazines produced by Colt.

Photo Jean Huon

Morgan Randle, a soldier of the 4th (Mechanized) Infantry Division fills his M 16 magazine.
Photo Jean Huon

Brownells, Montezuma (IA), Federal Ordnance Inc., South El Monte (CA), Lew Horton, Westboro (Minnesota), Parallex Corp., Chicago Ridge (IL), UA Magazines Inc., Downey (CA). Various attempts were made to produce magazines made of synthetic materials.

The first one we shall look at is the experimental model made by the chemical products division of General Electric.

It was a 20-round magazine which looked as though it was made of aluminum plate.

It was made of 'Lexan,' a polycarbonate resin. The rectangular elevator spring was replaced by two helical springs. It was tested in November 1966 but was not adopted by the Army.

More recently, Gapco of Wilson, South Carolina offered a magazine made of Zytel, a synthetic material produced by Dupont. It had a 30-round capacity and had a remodeled box shape with horizontal ribbing for reinforcement.

The Israeli firm Orlite (a division of Israel Aircraft Industries Ltd) also produced a magazine in composite material. It had a 30-round capacity, was made in high-resistance plastic reinforced with fiberglass and was molded in a single piece.

Black and transparent plastic magazines were also produced by Ram-Line, Eagle and Beta.

Diemaco of Canada fitted its C 7 and C 8 weapons with 30-round, plastic magazines made by Thermold.

Metal magazines of 20, 30 and 40 rounds.
Photo Jean Huon

Magazine cover

There was already a magazine cover for the US M 1 carbine. It was made of neoprene and repelled mud, dust and foreign bodies and found its way onto the M 16 magazine.

Cadet Lolita Malepai during firing training at Schofield Barracks, Ohio, March 23rd 1980.
Photo U.S. Army

Testing a 40-round magazine in Vietnam.
Author's Collection

Black plastic Orlite magazine.
Photo IMI

Ram-Line magazine.
It can be mounted on the M 16, the AR-18 or the Mini-14.
Photo Ram-Line

Transparent plastic Eagle magazine.
Photo Jean Huon

Black plastic Eagle magazine.
Photo Jean Huon

Three 30-round magazines mounted on the Tri-Mag.
Photo Maxwell G. Atchisson/Donald G. Thomas

Black composite material Thermold magazine.
Photo Jean Huon

Tri-Mag

Tri-Mag was one among Maxwell Atchisson's inventions. It consisted of three rectangular sleeves each holding a 30-round magazine.

This device had been invented to allow faster reloading and was recommended for the M 16 A1 machine gun with the Atchisson conversion.

The Tri-Mag mounted on an Atchisson machine gun.
Photo Maxwell G. Atchisson/Donald G. Thomas

The Tri-Mag has an auxiliary clip to assist in supporting the weapon's increased weight.
Photo Maxwell G. Atchisson/Donald G. Thomas

Redi-Mag

The Redi-Mag was a device which allowed a reserve magazine to be fitted alongside the one in the feed tube, ensuring faster reloading. It was put on the market by J.F.S. of Salem, Oregon.

High-capacity magazines

In 1981 Mack Gwinn invented a drum magazine with a 75-round capacity. Inspired by the Soviet RPK machine gun, it consisted of a plated, semi-conical case with transparent Lexan cover and a feed sleeve borrowed from a standard magazine.

This magazine was tested by the US Marines and it was distributed in the private sector by Phoenix Inc. of Boulder, Colorado.

The Tri-Mag holds 90 cartridges and weighs 450gm empty and 1470gm when full.
Photo Maxwell G. Atchisson/Donald G. Thomas

The M 16

It is possible to fit the M 16 with 50-100 round drum magazines designed for the Ultimax light machine gun, produced by Chartered Industries of Singapore. These magazines consist of a metallic box with a transparent base, which allows immediate observation of the filling level. They were sold in the USA by shooting accessory companies.

Beta Company of Tucker, Georgia, developed a 100-round magazine which they designated C-MAG. It consisted of two drums coupled together by a distributor which took the place of the standard magazine. It was largely made of composite material. There were also 90-round magazines, sold by Mitchell Arms.

Diemaco produced a 100-round drum magazine with the C 7 and C 8 derivatives arms collection.

Chinese manufactured drum magazines have a poor reputation and function badly.

Belt-feeding

To further increase the fire capacity of the M 16 there was a conversion unit which allowed the weapon to be belt fed. Developed by Jonathan Arthur Ciener, this mechanism required a modification of the frame. It could be fitted either to a rifle or a carbine version of the M 16. It was offered with a plastic casing which allowed a 100-round belt to be fitted.

▲
Belt feeding
Photo JAC.

◄
The Redi-Mag allows a spare magazine to be carried.
Photos JFS

▼

50 and 100 round drum magazines alongside 20 and 30 round box magazines.

Photo CIS

Maintenance equipment

Firing errors which could occur with the early versions of the M 16 A1 were largely due to insufficient cleaning.

This led the US Army to order a cleaning kit which comprised:
- a four-part cleaning rod,
- a rag-holder,
- a chamber brush,
- a barrel brush, pipe-cleaners to clear the outlet of the gas duct,
- a brush,
- an oil can.

This equipment was carried in a packet which could be fixed in the buttstock; an opening in the shoulder plate gave access to the cleaning compartment.

It could also be fitted in a kit, closed by Velcro and press-studs, fastened to the belt by a hook and eye.

The M 16 A2 was similarly equipped.

Bayonets

The M 16, M 16 A1 and M 16 A2 mounted various types of bayonets:
- The first AR-15s were made with a bayonet similar to the M 4 but with an enlarged ring. The grip and sheath were both made in olive green or blue plastic.
- M 7. This is derived from the M 3 combat knife and from the M 4 bayonet on the M 1 US carbine. Its leaf-shaped, double-edged blade is bronzed and it measures 167mm with a 22mm in diameter ring in the crosspiece. The grip is spindle-shaped and finished with finely-scored black plastic platelets. The M 8 A1 sheath is in olive green plastic with buckle and keeper in khaki netting. It also has a suspension hook which fitted the US eyeleted waistbelt. The M 7 bayonet could also be used on the AR-18 assault weapon.
- M 7 Long. Variation with 231mm blade.
- M 7 Experimental. Variation developed in 1974-75 with a Bowie knife blade, identical to that of the Marines' combat knife.
- KCB 70. A bayonet developed in 1973 in the Netherlands by NWM. It was modeled on the bayonets used for the Russian Kalashnikov. It consisted of a powerful 175mm Bowie blade in

The 100 round C-Mag magazine.

Photo Beta

chrome plate with a saw-tooth back edge. The upright crosspiece has a ring. The rectangular-sectioned handle was of black plastic. The sheath was of black polycarbonate, and at the upper end a steel-plated yoke was riveted to a keeper of khaki webbing which had a suspension hook and a safety catch with a press stud. The other end of the sheath is reinforced by a steel mount which consisted of a screwdriver blade, a notch and a teat. Fitting the blade on the end of the sheath produced a wire cutter.
- M 9. A bayonet put into service at the same time as the M 16 A2. It was developed by Phrobis Int'l. of Oceanside, California and was also made by Buck Knives and Marto. Covered by Patent No. 4.821.356, it had a stainless

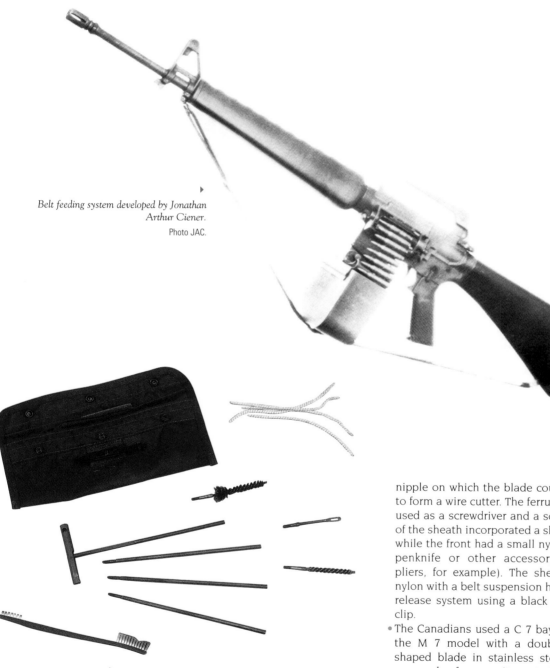

Belt feeding system developed by Jonathan Arthur Ciener.
Photo JAC.

Cleaning kit for the M 16 A1.
Photo Jean Huon

nipple on which the blade could be mounted to form a wire cutter. The ferrule could also be used as a screwdriver and a scraper. The back of the sheath incorporated a sharpening stone while the front had a small nylon pocket for a penknife or other accessory (Leatherman pliers, for example). The sheath-holder was nylon with a belt suspension hook and a rapid release system using a black plastic, flexible clip.

- The Canadians used a C 7 bayonet similar to the M 7 model with a double-edged, leaf-shaped blade in stainless steel. The casing was made of composite material with a Velcro fastening, nylon keeper and buckle. The C 7 bayonet was made by Nelle Cutlery Service of Stoney Creek, Ontario.

Bipod

To make shooting more accurate while prone, Colt developed a stand consisting of two aluminum legs which could be attached to the barrel on a level with the base of the cross-

steel 178mm Bowie blade with a single edge, the back serving as a saw. The crosspiece included a steel ring. The cylindrical, slotted handgrip was made of Zytel. The sheath was also of Zytel and equipped with a ferrule and a sight. A spring held this stand open while it was fitted to the weapon. Unfolded it was 28cm high and 30cm wide. It could be dismantled and carried in a belt case.

Another more recent stand, based on the same principle, was made of synthetic material. There are also other stands

• A folding model which can be attached to the front of the muzzle brake in the form of an articulated bridge with tubular arms reinforced by perforated plates. Weighing only 370gm, it is made of anodized aluminum and sold by Assault Systems of St Louis, Missouri. It is now installed on HBAR models by Colt.

• A light model known as the Featherweight is aimed at marksmen and formed a central or forward support depending on the end of the handguard to which it was fitted. It is distributed by Glaser of Forest City, California.

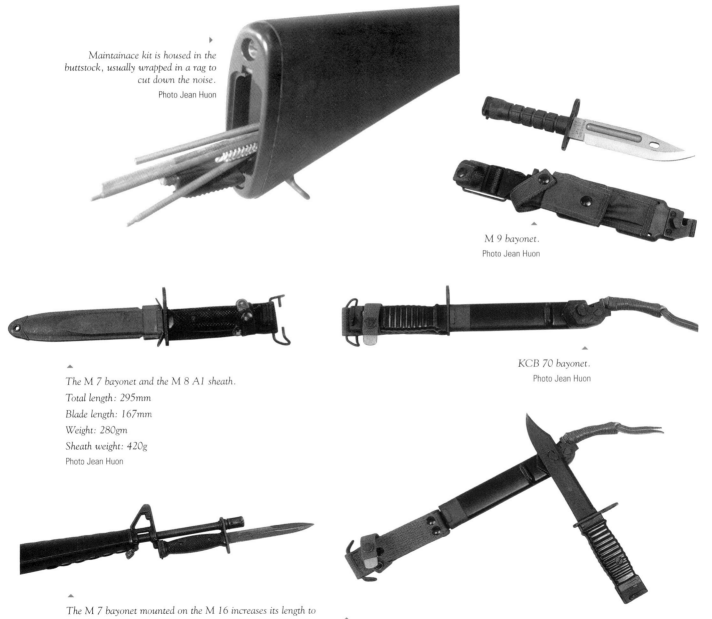

Maintainace kit is housed in the buttstock, usually wrapped in a rag to cut down the noise.
Photo Jean Huon

M 9 bayonet.
Photo Jean Huon

The M 7 bayonet and the M 8 A1 sheath.
Total length: 295mm
Blade length: 167mm
Weight: 280gm
Sheath weight: 420g
Photo Jean Huon

KCB 70 bayonet.
Photo Jean Huon

The M 7 bayonet mounted on the M 16 increases its length to 1.112 meters.
Photo Jean Huon

The KCB bayonet can be converted into a wire cutter.
Photo Jean Huon

Sight aids

The Combat Optical Gunsight was originally an Israeli accessory. It increases accuracy on a moving target by 30% at 250 meters and by 46% at 50 meters in the same conditions. It weighs only 360gm and its effective range is 300 meters.

- an adjustable plate with five eyelets, placed in the pistol grip (invented by John K Jorczak),
- a lateral sight bar introduced by Karl R Lewis,
- the XM 178 sight grid invented by Nicholas Sophinos, Robert D Fremont and Edward L Gallini,
- the M 203 sight grid.

A prone US soldier fires a precision shot with the M 16 A1 equipped with a bipod stand.
Photo Colt

Sight grids

A sight grid, which assists accuracy when firing finned grenades, can be fitted on the M 16. It is fitted in front of the cross-sight and does not interfere with the firing of cartridges because a small gap in the grid, level with the cross-sight, gives a clear field of fire.

There are other devices which can be fitted on the M 16:

Folding stand.
Photo Assault Systems

Night sight

Maxwell G Atchisson developed a night firing device for the M 16.

It was a sight bar on a stamped plate, which was fixed on the carrying handle, and which had a wide eyepiece and a cross-sight, the two being formed by a wafer and a luminous disc.

This device, like some other inventions of Maxwell Atchisson's, did not get beyond the prototype stage.

Volley limiter

On September 30, 1971 Colt registered (under US Patent No. 850.2142) a volley limiter which could be fitted to the M 16.

The trigger system was replaced with a completely different mechanism using a cam and two or three cogs and all of which was done without otherwise modifying the weapon.

It made it possible to fire limited shots or volleys of two or three rounds while the selector was in place.

▲

Elbits Computers' sighting system.
Photo Elbits

It was only after the adoption of the M 16 A2 that the three-shot selector was taken up by the US Army.

The free volley option was still available for export. Though not kept by the US Army, the device still appears in Colt's export catalog.

There were further volley-limiting projects, among which were:
- one developed by Gene Stoner after 1959 (Patent No. 3.045.555, July 24th 1962),
- another by Forster E. Sturtevant, a Colt technician (US Patent No. 3.292.492, December 20th 1966).

Rate of fire limiters

Among the many attempts which had been made to improve the M 16 it is important to note the devices intended to slow the rate of fire in order to achieve greater precision.

Forster E Sturtevant, the Colt technician mentioned above, invented an inhibitor which worked on the firing mechanism by slowing the action of the hammer on the percussor after the breech is closed and locked.

This mechanism could be moved in and out of gear by means of the selector, giving the user the option of normal or slow fire. It is covered by Patent No. 3.301.133, January 31st 1967.

D Stoehr of TRW Systems Group, Redondo Beach, California had a completely different idea. It worked by replacing the flash suppressor with a conical muzzle brake with three or four vents. To reduce the rate of fire to about 400 rounds per minute and to improve the weapon's precision, other alterations were made:
- increasing the weight of the moving part,
- shortening the recuperator spring,
- enlarging the vent,
- replacing the plastic buttstock with one in tubular metal whose shoulder plate was in the

▼

The Elbits system is fitted on most Israeli M 16s.
Photo Tzahal (IDF)

Sighting grid for finned missiles.
Photo Colt

Atchisson night firing mechanism for the M 16.
Photo Maxwell G. Atchisson/Donald G. Thomas

tubular metal whose shoulder plate was in the axis of the barrel,
- mounting a Single Point sight,
- using cartridges underloaded by 20% and armed with lighter bullets.

Tri-Burst

Rather than reducing the rate or fire, Orpheus Industries' (of Montrose, Colorado) Tri-Burst was a mechanical system which allowed semi-automatic weapons to be fired in sequences of three quick-fire rounds.

On the AR-15 the Tri-Burst mechanism could be installed in replacement of the detachable part of the trigger guard.

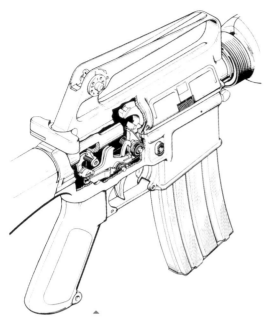

Blank firing cartridge plugs

To allow the M 16 to fire blank cartridges automatically, a plug must be fitted at the end of the barrel.

This partially seals the flash-suppressor and maintains the pressure in the barrel needed to rest the bolt.

There are two models of these plugs: one from Colt is in the form of a cylinder fitted to the flash suppressor by means of a sliding hook. A weak tip is broken if a live cartridge is fired in error.

The US Army plug is cube-shaped. It is attached to the weapon by means of an extendable foot inserted in the flash suppressor and fixed there by a thumbscrew. This device does not allow firing of live cartridges.

Both of these blank firing cartridge plugs are painted red.

Volley fire limiter installed on the M 16.
Document Colt

The Tri-Burst is an accessory which permits the practical speed of fire of a semi-automatic weapon to be increased.
Document Tri-Burst

The M 16

Blank firing plug developed by Colt for export models of the M 16.
Document Colt

Regulation blank firing plug.
Photo Jean Huon

Rangers training with the blank firing plug fitted on the M 16. Note the camouflaged weapons.
Photo U.S. Army

Safety plugs

There are two models (one red, one black) of safety plugs. They cap the flash suppressor and keep both water and foreign bodies out of the barrel.

Noise suppressors for the M 16

There are several models of silencer for the M 16 developed in the USA by Sionic Noise and others.

In Sweden, Interdynamic AB brought out a silencer which was intended to be used on the M 16. It was a baffle noise regulator derived from one invented by Hiram Maxim at the start of the twentieth century. It took the form of a cylinder which was screwed on to the end of the barrel in place of the flash suppressor. Interdynamic developed, in parallel with this silencer, a special subsonic cartridge whose use

This soldier is carrying an M 16 fitted with a blank fire plug during an exercise in Australia.
Photo U.S. Army.

Stopper plug for the M 16 flame suppressor.
Photo Jean Huon

was vital if the weapon was to be used properly with the noise suppressor. The brass case had an internal plastic sleeve which reduced the volume of the powder chamber.

The charge is clearly less powerful than that of a normal cartridge. The bullet is cylindrical, weighs 5.3gm and has a dummy plastic cap. To use them with the M 16 a special magazine is needed. The weapon will only fire single shots and needs reloading after each shot.

The firm of Stopson in France also developed several models of silencer for the M 16.

Weight reducing kit

Future Industries of San José, California produce a kit which enables the weight of the M 16 to be reduced by about 500gm. The handguard is replaced by a black plastic, perforated tube. The cross-sight mount has to be removed before this one-piece part can be fitted.

The hollow triangular buttstock is of light alloy and consists of a cylindrical element placed around the tube of the recuperator spring and a shoulder plate fitted with a reinforced stalk.

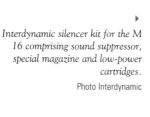

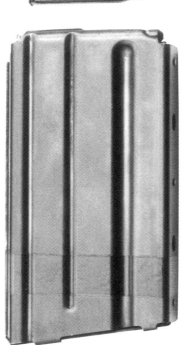

Interdynamic silencer kit for the M 16 comprising sound suppressor, special magazine and low-power cartridges.
Photo Interdynamic

M 16 with Interdynamic silencer.
Photo Interdynamic

Stopson silencer fitted on an M 16 derivative.
Photo Stopson

M 16 with the Future Industries weight reducing kit.
Photo James T. Carpenter

The M 16

Recoil compensator

With the aim of reducing the recoil of the M 16 an inventor named Mack Gwinn produced a muzzle brake based on that of the Soviet AK-74 assault rifle.

It consisted of a cylindrical decompression chamber with lateral vents.

This accessory, which was marketed by Phoenix Inc. of Boulder, Colorado at a price of $32, reduced the recoil of the M 16 by around 65%-70%.

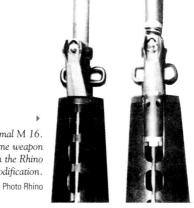

Left: Normal M 16.
Right: The same weapon
with the Rhino
modification.
Photo Rhino

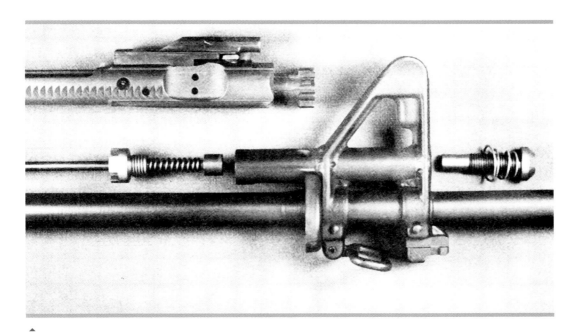

Rhino blowback system.
Photo Rhino

Chemical detector

A detection device capable of registering the presence of the enemy, by recognizing chemicals emitted by human breath, can be mounted at the end of the M 16.

New blowback

Rhino International Corp. of Lansdowne, Pennsylvania tested an interesting idea by substituting a cylinder and piston system for the blowback supply tube. A gas cylinder is welded over the hoop and locks a piston, whose length is increased by a rod and which acts directly on the breech. The cylinder contains a release spring and a shock absorber. The whole is made up of only twelve parts and increases the weight of the weapon by a mere 50gm.

When the shot is fired the piston recoils by about 12mm and hits the breech with enough force to unlock the moving head and open the breech. This is based on the same short-stroke principle employed in the US M1 carbine. An escape valve is placed facing the piston which, because of its position, allows some of the gas to escape. By this means it is possible to reduce the rate of fire to 450 rounds per minute, two-round bursts can be obtained and accuracy is improved.

Cheek rest for either rifle or carbine, developed by Glaser.
Photo Glaser

Cheek rest

A Glaser accessory makes it possible to install a cheek rest on the M 16 or the carbine to ease the discomfort of the firer.

Straps

The M 16 is usually provided with a conventional, black nylon strap.

There is also a Redi-Tac assault strap which enables the weapon to be carried crosswise or on the shoulder. It is marketed by J.F.S. Inc.

The M 16

The Redi-Tac allows a weapon to be
carried crosswise or on the shoulder.
Photo JFS

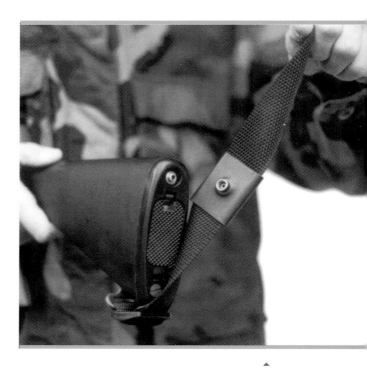

The Redi-Tac is held in an upright position
by means of a press stud.
Photo JFS

At the beginning of the war in Vietnam the same webbing was used for both the M 16 and the M 14, with two side pockets for
grenades. Combatants also carried bandoliers fitted with loaded magazines.
Author's Collection

Cartridge Bags

When the M 16 went into service the rigid webbing cartridge pouches carrying two M 14 or two 20-round M 16 magazines (three if absolutely necessary) were supplied.

They were fitted with a strap which was fixed to the belt with hooks and they closed with a webbing tongue which went into a metal clip.

On each side of the pouch, fasteners allowed grenades to be attached. On the inside face of the strap, in FSN/NSN nomenclature, name and number were marked:

CASE, SMALL ARMS, AMMUNITION
DSA – 1 – 8682 – 8465 – 647- 0852

Later a flexible nylon pouch was used. This closed with a black plastic clasp and carried four 20-round magazines. It was fitted with a pull strip easing the extraction of the magazines. Its side faces were fitted to carry two grenades. On the inside of the flap was printed:

CASE, AMMUNITION, M 16
20 ROUND MAGAZINE
DSA 100-68-C27788466-935-6780

A new cartridge pouch, similar but taller, appeared with the advent of 30-round magazines. The pull string was abandoned and, depending on the model, there were two means of keeping the magazines in place; either separating ribbons or individual flaps with metal ends.

▲
Sergeant Hector Diaz of the Big Red One tries out the new 30-round magazine and its pouch at Fort Benning in May 1970.
Photo U.S. Army

▲
Vietnamese soldier with an M 16 A1 and with M 14 cartridge pouches in 1971.
Author's Collection

The cartridge pouch had semi-rigid plastic reinforcement on the back and front and on the front face of the flap.

It was not systematically marked with the NSN number but those which were had this:

CASE, SMALL ARMS AMMUNITION,
M 16 RIFLE FOR 3 30 ROUND MAGAZINE
8465-00-001-8452

There are indications of the existence of another webbing cartridge, which took two 20-round magazines side by side in separate pockets. This is rather like an up-scale version of the magazine pouch for the Colt M 1911. Despite research by our US correspondents, no

NSN number has been found for this equipment.

Carrying Bag

For transport in humid or dusty areas the M 16 can be placed in a transparent plastic bag closed with a rubber band.

M 16 20-round magazine pouch.
Photo Jean Huon

M 14 magazine pouch.
Photo Jean Huon

M 16 30-round magazine pouch.
Photo Jean Huon

1. INSERT RIFLE IN BAG.
2. FOLD BAG OVER AND AROUND BUTTSTOCK.
3. INSTALL RUBBER BAND OVER BUTTSTOCK AND BAG.
4. TO QUICKLY REMOVE RIFLE, GRASP RIFLE BY PISTOL GRIP AND SNAP TOP OF BAG AWAY FROM BOTTOM OF BAG.

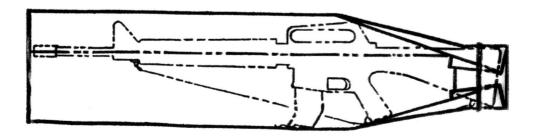

The method for stowing the M 16 in its carrying pouch is stenciled on the plastic.
Photo Jean Huon

Summary tables of M 16 variants produced by Colt

The number of variations of the M 16 made by Colt is impossible to count; given the modular design of the weapon it is possible to adapt each variation to an individual client.

It is difficult to detail all these in a work of this kind but the following tables will give a general idea of the principal variations which are on file.

The M 16 A1 is the weapon with by far the most widespread use.
Author's Collection

The M 16

Ref.	Model	Observations
231	Port Firing Weapon U.S. Army	Gun port weapon, designed to be fired from behind light armor. No button closure. No sights.
601 R 6000	AR 15 Sporter Commercial	Semi-automatic.Frame without button closure. Sight adjustable for drift. Light 0.508 meter barrel with 12-inch rifling. Manufactured 1964-1985.
R 6001	AR 15 Carbine	Semi-automatic. Frame without button closure. Telescoping buttstock. Sight adjustable for drift. 0.508 meter barrel with 12-inch rifling. Manufactured 1977-1985.
602	AR 15 U.S. Gov. Issue	Semi-auto. Frame without button closure. Sight adjustable for drift. 0.508 meter barrel with 12-inch rifling.
603	M 16 A1 (ex XM 16 E1)	Selective fire. Frame with button closure. Sight adjustable for drift. 0.508 meter barrel with 12-inch rifling.
604	M 16 U.S. Air Force	Selective fire. Frame without button closure. Sight adjustable for drift. 0.508 meter barrel with 12-inch rifling.
605 A	M 16 Carbine	Selective fire. Frame without button closure. Sight adjustable for drift. Fixed buttstock.
605 B	M 16 Carbine	Selective fire with 3-round volley limiter. Frame with button closure. Sight adjustable for drift. Fixed buttstock.
606	HBAR	Selective fire. Frame without button closure. Sight adjustable for drift. Heavy 0.508 meter barrel with 12-inch rifling. Bipod
606 A	HBAR	Selective fire. Frame with button closure. Sight adjustable for drift. Heavy barrel.
606 B	HBAR	Selective fire with 3-round volley limiter. Frame with button closure. Sight adjustable for drift. Heavy barrel.
607	5.56 mm Sub-machine gun	Telescoping buttstock. 0.254 meter barrel.
608	CAR 15	Survival rifle with 0.254 meter barrel. Fixed tubular buttstock.
609	XM 177 E1	Selective fire. Frame with button closure. Sight adjustable for drift. Telescopic buttstock. 0.254 meter rifling with 12-inch rifling.
610	XM 177 U.S. Air Force	Selective fire. Frame without button closure. Sight adjustable for drift. Telescoping buttstock. 0.154 meter barrel with 12-inch rifling.
610 B	5.56 mm Sub-machine gun	Selective fire. Frame with button closure. Sight adjustable for drift. Telescopic buttstock. 0.254 meter barrel with 12-inch rifling.
611	HBAR	Export model of 606.

Ref.	Model	Observations
613	M 16 A1	Export model of 603.
614	AR-15	Export model of 603 without button closure.
616	Machine Gun	Export model of 604
619	5.56mm Machine Pistol	Export Model of 609
620	5.56mm Machine Pistol	Export model of 610.
621	Machine Gun	Export model of 603.
R 6222	AR 15	.22 Long Rifle conversion kit. Manufactured from 1990.
629	XM 177 E2 U.S. Army	Selective fire. Frame with button closure. Sight adjustable for drift. Telescoping buttstock. 0.292 meter barrel with 12-inch rifling.
630	5.56mm Machine Pistol U.S. Air Force	Selective fire. Frame with button closure. Sight adjustable for drift. Telescoping buttstock. 0.292 meter barrel with 12-inch rifling.
633	9mm Machine Pistol	Selective fire. Sight adjustable for drift. 0.228 meter barrel with 12-inch rifling. Mechanical shock absorber.
633 HB	9mm Machine Pistol	Selective fire. Sight adjustable for drift. 0.228 meter barrel with 12-inch rifling. Hydraulic shock absorber.
634	9mm Machine Pistol	Selective fire. Sight adjustable for drift. 0.228 meter barrel with 12-inch rifling. Chamber and bore chrome plated.
635	9mm Machine Pistol	Selective fire. Sight adjustable for drift. 0.254 meter barrel with 10-inch rifling. Chamber and bore chrome plated.
639	9mm Machine Pistol	Selective fire with limiter. Sight adjustable for drift. 0.254 meter barrel with 12-inch rifling. Chamber and bore chrome plated.
640	5.56mm Machine Pistol	Similar to model 639 but with button closure.
R 6420	AR 15 Carbine	Semi-auto. Frame with button closure. Sight adjustable for drift. Telescopic buttstock. Light 0.409 meter barrel with 7-inch rifling. Manufactured 1985 - 1987
R 6430	9mm Sporter Carbine	Semi-auto. A1 type sight. Telescoping buttstock. 0.409 meter barrel with 10-inch rifling. Produced from 1992.

Ref.	Model	Observations
645	M16 A2	Selective fire. Type A2 body. Frame with button closure. Type A2 sight. Heavy 0.508 meter barrel with 7-inch rifling. Chamber and bore chrome plated.
645 E	M 16 A2	Semi-automatic. Type A2 body. Frame with button closure ratcheted above. 0.508 meter barrel with 7-inch rifling.
R 6450	AR 15 9 mm Carbine	Semi-automatic. Type A2 sight. Telescoping buttstock. 0.409 meter barrel with 10-inch rifling. Produced from 1985.
649	9 mm Sub-machine gun U.S. Air Force	Selective fire. Frame with button closure. Sight adjustable for drift. Telescoping buttstock. 0.241 meter barrel with 12-inch rifling.
R 6500	AR 15 A2	Semi-automatic. Frame with button closure. Sight adjustable for drift. 0.508 meter barrel with 7-inch rifling. Produced from 1984-1988.
651	M 16 A1 Carbine	Selective fire. Frame with button closure. Sight adjustable for drift. 0.368 meter barrel with 12-inch rifling. Fixed buttstock.
R 6510	AR 15 A2	Variant of R6500 converted for .222 Remington.
652	M 16 A1 Carbine	Selective fire. Frame without button closure. Type A2 sight. Telescoping buttstock. 0.368 meter barrel with 12-inch rifling.
R 6520	M 16 A2 Carbine	Selective fire. Type A2 body. Type A2 sight. Light 0.409 meter barrel with 7-inch rifling. Produced from 1988.
653	M 16 A1 Carbine	Selective fire. Frame with button closure. Sight adjustable for drift. Telescoping buttstock. 0.368 meter barrel with 12-inch rifling.
654	M 16 Carbine	Frame without button closure. Telescoping buttstock. 0.368 meter barrel.
6520	AR 1502 Government Carbine	Semi-auto. Type A2 body. Frame without button closure. Type A2 sight. Telescoping buttstock. 0.409 meter barrel with 7-inch rifling. Chamber and bore chrome plated.
6530	AR 15 Government Carbine	Semi-auto. Type A2 body. Frame with button closure. Type A2 sight. 0.402 meter barrel with 7-inch rifling. Chamber and bore chrome plated.
MT 6530	Match Target Lightweight	Semi-auto. Type A2 body. Frame with button closure. Type A2 sight. 0.409 meter barrel with 7-inch rifling.
655	M 16 A1 Sniper	Experimental model with body modified to incorporate a telescope.

Ref.	Model	Observations
R 6550	AR 15 A2	Semi-automatic. Type A2 body. Frame with button closure. Type A2 sight. 0.508 meter barrel with 7-inch rifling. Produced from 1988-1990.
R 6550	AR 15 A2	Semi-automatic. Type A2 body. Frame with button closure. Type A2 sight. 0.508 meter barrel with 7-inch rifling. Produced from 1988-1990.
R 6551 or MT 6551	Match Target or Sporter Target	Semi-automatic. Type A2 body. Frame with button closure. Type A2 sight. 0.508 meter barrel with 7-inch rifling. Produced from 1991.
656	M 16 A1 Sniper	Experimental model with body adapted to take a telescope. Barrel fitted with noise suppressor.
R 6600	AR 15 A2 HBAR	Semi-auto. Type A2 body. Frame with button closure. Type A2 sight. 0.508 meter barrel with 7-inch rifling. Produced from 1986-1991.
R 6600 DH	Sporter Match Delta HBAR	Semi-auto. Type A2 body. Frame with button closure. Type A2 sight. 0.508 meter heavy barrel with 7-inch rifling. Produced from 1987-1990.
R 6601 or MT 6601	Target HBAR Rifle	Semi-auto. Type A2 body. Frame with button closure. Type A2 sight. 0.508 meter heavy barrel with 7-inch rifling. Produced from 1992.
R 6700 or MT 6700	Match Target HBAR	Semi-automatic. Type A2 body. Frame with button closure and ratcheted top with Type A2 sight and fixed carrying handle. 0.508 meter barrel with 9-inch rifling. Produced from 1992.
R 6700 CH	Sporter Competition HBAR	Semi-automatic. Type A2 body. Frame with button closure and ratcheted top with Type A2 sight and fixed carrying handle. Heavy 0.508 meter barrel with 9-inch rifling. Produced from 1992.
R 6700 DC or MT 6700	Sporter Conversion Kit	Semi-auto. Type A2 body. Frame with button closure and ratcheted top with Type A2 sight and fixed carrying handle. Heavy 0.508 meter barrel with 9-inch rifling. Produced from 1993.
6724	Colt's Accurized Rifle	Semi-automatic. Type A2 body. Frame with button closure and ratcheted top with telescopic sight. 0.61 meter heavy barrel in stainless steel with 9-inch rifling. Free floating barrel.

Ref.	Model	Observations
6731	Match Target Competition II HBAR Rifle	Semi-automatic. Type A2 body. Frame with button closure and ratcheted top with Type A2 sight and fixed carrying handle. 0.508 meter barrel with 9-inch rifling.
R 6830	Sporter Lightweight	Semi-automatic. Type A2 body. Frame with button closure and ratcheted top with Telescopic sight. Heavy 0.409 meter barrel with 7-inch rifling. Chambered in 7.62 x 39 Produced from 1993.
R 6850 DC or MT 6850 DC	Sporter Conversion Kit	Semi-automatic. Type A2 body. Frame with button closure and ratcheted top with telescopic sight. Light 0.409 meter barrel with 7-inch rifling. Chambered in 7.62 x 39 Produced from 1993.
R 6851 DC or MT 6851 DC	Sporter Conversion Kit	Semi-automatic. Type A2 body. Frame with button closure and ratcheted top with telescopic sight. Light 0.508 meter barrel with 7-inch rifling. Chambered in 7.62 x 39 Produced from 1993.
R 6900 DC or MT 6900 DC	Sporter Conversion Kit,	Semi-automatic. Type A2 body. Frame with button closure. Type A2 sight. Light 0.508 meter barrel with 7-inch rifling. Produced from 1993.
6920	Law Enforcement Carbine	Semi-automatic. Type A2 body. Frame with button closure and ratcheted top with Type A2 sight and fixed carrying handle. Telescoping buttstock. 0.409 meter barrel with chrome plated chamber and bore. Barrel adapted for M 203 grenade launcher.
6921	M 4 LE	Semi-auto. Type A2 body. Frame with button closure and ratcheted top with Type A2 sight and fixed carrying handle. Telescoping buttstock. 0.409 meter barrel with 7-inch rifling. Chamber and bore in chrome plate. Barrel adapted for M 203 grenade launcher.
701	M 16 A2	Selective fire. Type A2 body. Frame with button closure. Type A2 sight. Light 0.506 meter barrel with 7-inch rifling. Chamber and bore in chrome plate.
702	M 16 A2	Selective fire. Type A2 body. Frame with button closure. Sight adjustable for drift. Heavy 0.508 meter barrel with 7-inch rifling.
703	M 16 A2	Selective fire. Type A2 body. Frame with button closure. Type A2 sight. Light 0.508 meter barrel with 7-inch rifling.
705	M 16 A2 E3	Selective fire. Type A2 body. Frame with button closure. Type A2 sight. Heavy 0.508 meter barrel with 7-inch rifling.

Ref.	Model	Observations
707	M 16 A2	Selective fire with 3-round volley limiter. Type A2 body. Frame with button closure. Type A2 sight. Light 0.508 meter barrel with 12-inch rifling.
711	C 7 Canadian	Selective fire. Frame with button closure. Sight adjustable for drift. Light 0.508 meter barrel with 12-inch rifling.
713	M 16 A2	Selective fire with 3-round volley limiter. Type A2 body. Frame with button closure. Sight adjustable for drift. Light 0.508 meter barrel with 7-inch rifling.
715	M 16 A2	Selective fire with 3-round volley limiter. Type A2 body. Frame with button closure. Type A2 sight. Heavy 0.508 meter barrel with 7-inch rifling.
719	M 16 A2	Selective fire with 3-round volley limiter. Type A2 body. Frame with button closure. Sight adjustable for drift. Light 0.508 meter barrel with 7-inch rifling.
720	M 4 Carbine	Selective fire with 3-round volley limiter. Type A2 body. Frame with button closure and top ratcheted with Type A2 sight and fixed carrying handle. Heavy 0.368 meter barrel with 7-inch rifling and chrome plated chamber and bore.
723	M 16 A2 Carbine Delta Force	Selective fire. Frame with button closure. Sight adjustable for drift. Telescoping buttstock. 0.368 meter barrel with 7-inch rifling.
725	C 8 Canadian	Selective fire with 3-round volley limiter. Frame with button closure. Sight adjustable for drift. Telescoping buttstock. 0.368 meter barrel with 7-inch rifling.
725 A	M 16 A2 Carbine	Selective fire with 3-round volley limiter. Frame with button closure. Sight adjustable for drift. Telescoping buttstock. Light 0.368 meter barrel with 7-inch rifling.
725 B	M 16 A2 Carbine	Selective fire with 3-round volley limiter. Frame with button closure. Sight adjustable for drift. Telescoping buttstock. Heavy 0.368 meter barrel with 7-inch rifling.
727	M 16 A2 Carbine U.S. Navy	Selective fire. Frame with button closure. Sight adjustable for drift. Telescoping buttstock. 0.368 meter barrel with 7-inch rifling. Barrel adapted for M 203 grenade launcher.
728	M 16 A2 Carbine	Selective fire. Frame with button closure. Sight adjustable for drift. Telescoping buttstock. 0.368 meter barrel with 7-inch rifling. Barrel adapted for M 203 grenade launcher.
729	M 16 A2 Carbine	Selective fire with 3-round volley limiter. Frame with button closure. Sight adjustable for drift. Telescoping buttstock. 0.368 meter barrel with 7-inch rifling. Barrel adapted for M 203 grenade launcher.

M 16 A3 *Carbine*.
Photo Jean-Louis Courtois

Ref.	Model	Observations
733	M 16 A2 Commando	Selective fire. Type A2 body. Frame with button closure. Sight adjustable for drift. Telescoping buttstock. 0.368 meter barrel with 7-inch rifling. Chamber and bore chrome plated.
733 A	M 16 A2 Commando	Selective fire with 3-round volley limiter. Type A2 body. Frame with button closure. Sight adjustable for drift. Telescoping buttstock. 0.368 meter barrel with 7-inch rifling. Chamber and bore chrome plated.
735	M 16 A2 Commando	Selective fire with 3-round volley limiter. Type A2 body. Frame with button closure. Sight adjustable for drift. Telescoping buttstock. 0.292 meter barrel with 7-inch rifling. Chamber and bore chrome plated.
737	M 16 A2 HBAR Rifle	Selective fire. Sight adjustable for drift. 0.508 meter barrel with 7-inch rifling. Bipod stand.

Ref.	Model	Observations
741	M 16 A2 HBAR Rifle	Selective fire. Sight adjustable for height and drift. 0.508 meter barrel with 7-inch rifling. Bipod stand.
742	M 16 A2 HBAR Rifle	Selective fire. Sight adjustable for height and drift. 0.508 meter barrel with 7-inch rifling. Bipod stand.
745	M 16 A2 HBAR Rifle	Selective fire with 3-round volley limiter. Sight adjustable for height and drift. 0.508 meter barrel with 7-inch rifling. No stand.
746	M 16 A2 HBAR Rifle	Selective fire with 3-round volley limiter. Sight adjustable for height and drift. Heavy 0.508 meter barrel with 7-inch rifling. Bipod stand.
750	M 16 A2 HBAR Rifle	Automatic fire. Sight adjustable for height and drift. Heavy 0.508 meter barrel with 7-inch rifling. Bipod stand.
777	M 16 A4 Carbine	Selective fire. Telescopic buttstock. 0.368 meter barrel with 7-inch rifling. Chamber and bore in chrome plate. Barrel adapted for M 203 grenade launcher
779	M 16 A4 Carbine	Selective fire with 3-round volley limiter. Telescoping buttstock. 0.368 meter barrel with 7-inch rifling. Chamber and bore in chrome plate. Barrel adapted for M 203 grenade launcher.
901	M 16 A3	Automatic fire. Type A2 body. Frame with button closure and top ratcheted with Type A2 sight and fixed carrying handle. Heavy 0.508 barrel with 7-inch rifling. Chamber and bore chrome plated.
905	M 16 A3	Selective fire with 3-round volley limiter. Frame with button closure and ratcheted top with Type A2 sight and fixed carrying handle. Heavy 0.508 meter barrel with 7-inch rifling. Chamber and bore in chrome plate
925	M 16 A3 Carbine	Selective fire with 3-round volley limiter. Frame with button closure. Sight adjustable for drift. Telescoping buttstock. 0.368 meter barrel with 7-inch rifling.
927	M 4 A1 Carbine Special Forces	Selective fire. Frame with button closure and ratcheted top with Type A2 sight and fixed carrying handle. Telescoping buttstock. 0.368 meter barrel with 7-inch rifling. Barrel adapted for M 203 grenade launcher.
933	M 16 A2 Commando	Selective fire. Telescoping buttstock. Type A2 body. Frame with button closure and ratcheted top with Type A2 sight and fixed carrying handle. 0.292 meter barrel with 7-inch rifling. Chamber and bore in chrome plate.
935	M 16 A2 Commando	Selective fire with 3-round volley limiter. Telescoping buttstock. Frame with button closure and ratcheted top with Type A2 sight and fixed carrying handle. 0.292 meter barrel with 7-inch rifling. Chamber and bore in chrome plate.

The M 16

Ref.	Model	Observations
941	M 16 A3 HBAR Rifle	Selective fire. Ratcheted top with Type A2 sight and fixed carrying handle. 0.508 meter barrel with 7-inch rifling. Bipod stand.
942	M 16 A3 HBAR Rifle	Automatic fire. Ratcheted top with Type A2 sight and fixed carrying handle. 0.508 meter barrel with 7-inch rifling. Bipod stand.
950	M 16 A3 HBAR Rifle	Automatic fire. Ratcheted top with Type A2 sight and fixed carrying handle. 0.508 meter barrel with 7-inch rifling. Bipod stand.
977	M 16 A4 Carbine	Selective fire. Telescoping buttstock. Type A2 body. Frame with button closure and ratcheted top with Type A2 sight and fixed carrying handle. 0.368 meter barrel with 7-inch rifling. Chamber and bore in chrome plate. Barrel adapted for M 203 grenade launcher.
979	M 16 A4 Carbine	Selective fire with 3-round volley limiter. Telescoping buttstock. Type A2 body. Frame with button closure. Ratcheted top with Type A2 sight and fixed carrying handle. 0.368 meter barrel with 7-inch rifling. Chamber and bore in chrome plate. Barrel adapted for M 203 grenade launcher.

In 1967 the US Government acquired the license to produce the M 16 from Colt. Production was entrusted to Harrington & Richardson and to the Hydra-Matic Division of General Motors so as to diversify the suppliers of the US Army.

In addition Colt had given production licenses to other countries (on which subject the Hartford firm remains tight-lipped).

CANADA

Having tested the HK-11, the FNC, the M 16 A2 and the XL 64 E5, Canada stayed with the US weapon. Production was undertaken by Diemaco of Kitchener, Ontario, a private firm of the Héroux Devtek Group, which ensured both the production and the maintenance of the Canadian Army's light weapons. Canada adopted the C 7 assault rifle and the C 8 Carbine. Diemaco also offered a complete weapons system from the one basic model:

- **C 7 Rifle**. Essentially an M 16 A2 with right and left handed selector operation, a redesigned pistol grip, medium weight barrel, simplified sight, selector allowing single-shot or volley fire, a 30-round nylon magazine, four buttstock styles and a bayonet similar to the M 7 but with a stainless steel blade.
- **C 7 FT Rifle**. The carrying handle was replaced by a top plate taking an optical sight.
- **C 7 CT Rifle**. Long barrel with optical sight and stand.
- **C 8 Carbine.** With Telescoping buttstock.

◄
C 7 Assault rifle.
Photo Diemaco

◄
C 7 FT Marksman's rifle.
Photo Diemaco

◄
C 7 FT Competition rifle.
Photo Diemaco

The M 16

SFW Automatic carbine with 40mm M 203
grenade launcher.
M 203 de 40 mm.

C 7 CT Competition rifle.
Photo Diemaco

C 7 FT Marksman's rifle.
Photo Diemaco

Specifications	C 7	C 8
Caliber	5.56 mm	5.56 mm
Ammunition	5.56 mm NATO	5.56 mm NATO
Total length with buttstock extended	1.000 meter	0.760 meter
Total length with buttstock retracted	-	0.650 meter
Barrel length	0.500 meter	0.360 meter
Weight without magazine	3.400 kg	2.700 kg
Magazine capacity	30 rounds	30 rounds
Rate of fire	700-900 rounds/minute	750-950 rounds/mn

- **C 8 FT Carbine**. Variation of C 7 FT with telescoping buttstock.
- **C 8 FT HB Carbine**. Variation of the above with heavy barrel.
- **C 8 CT Carbine.** Telescoping buttstock, long barrel, optical sight and stand.
- **SFW** (Special Forces Weapons). Telescoping buttstock, optical sight, long barrel and M 203 grenade launcher.
- **SFSW** (Special Forces Support Weapon). Telescoping buttstock, optical sight, long barrel, carrying handle, stand and 100-round drum magazine.

- **LSW** (Light Support Weapon). Heavy barrel, carrying handle, optical sight and stand.
- **LSW99** (Improved Light Support Weapon). Similar to the above but with drum magazine.

Diemaco also manufactured M 203 grenade launchers and the 7.62 'Chain Gun' machine gun.

Some of Diemaco's production was exported (to Denmark, The Netherlands, Norway and the United Kingdom).

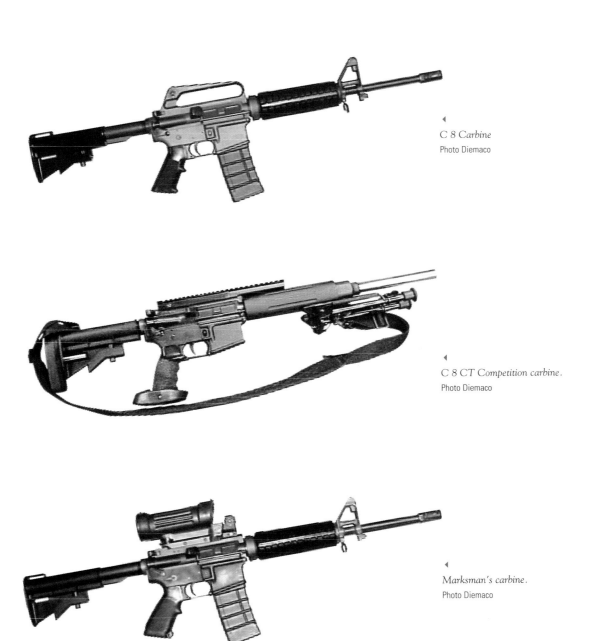

C 8 Carbine
Photo Diemaco

C 8 CT Competition carbine.
Photo Diemaco

Marksman's carbine.
Photo Diemaco

The M 16

CHINA

The firm Norinco manufactured many copies of western weapons (Colt M 1911 A1, M 14, FAMAS) without license. The M 16 suffered a similar fate and a Type 311 rifle was made in Beijing, which was very similar to the M 16 A1.

It featured a ribbed, cylindrical handguard, a contoured pistol grip and a semi-pistol stock.

PHILIPPINES

Elisco Tool in the Philippines produces several versions of the M 16. They are designated:
- M 613 P for the M 16 A1,
- M 611 P for the HBAR,
- M 653 P for the 368mm-barrel M 16 A1 carbine.

Philippines M 16s have the following marks:
- On the left: Made by Elisco Tool for the

Specifications	Singapore SAR-80
Caliber	5.56mm
Ammunition	5.56 x 45
Total length with buttstock extended	0.970 meter
Total length with buttstock retracted	0.738 meter
Barrel length	0.459 meter
Weight without magazine	3.700kg
Magazine capacity	20-30 rounds
Rate of fire	600-800 rounds/minute

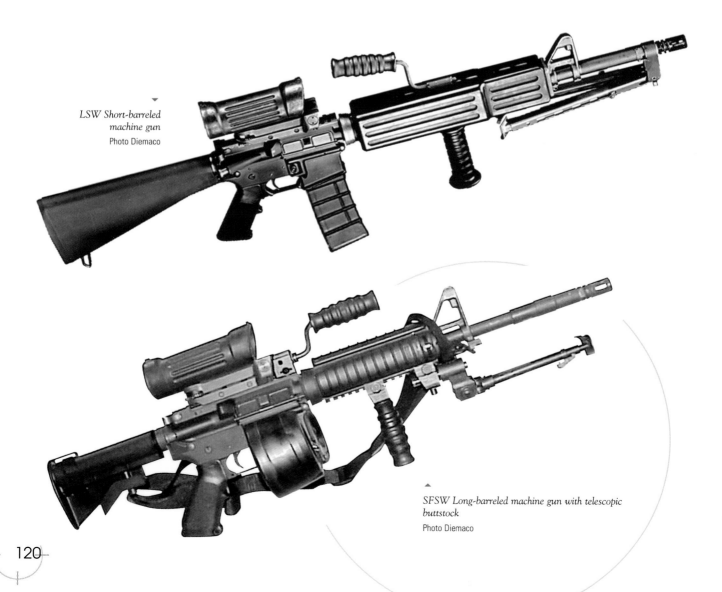

LSW Short-barreled machine gun
Photo Diemaco

SFSW Long-barreled machine gun with telescopic buttstock
Photo Diemaco

Republic of the Philippines, M 16 A1, RP00000
- On the right: Made in the Philippines under license from Colt's, Hartford, CT USA

SINGAPORE

Chartered Industries of Singapore obtained a license to produce the M 16.

This firm produced the AR-18 assault rifle and also developed a weapon combining the M 16 and the AR-18.

This was the SAR-80, developed jointly by CIS and the UK firm Sterling. It has conventional gas blowback with a piston-operated bolt.

The recuperator spring is housed in the breech behind the moving part. The arrangement of the bolt, the firing mechanism and the magazine are as on the M 16.

The SAR-80 is offered with either a fixed plastic buttstock or a tubular one which can be swiveled sideways.

SOUTH KOREA

Manufacture of the M 16 A1 in South Korea was undertaken by the Pusan Arsenal from 1963. Subsequently production was transferred to Daewoo.

The Korean M 16 A1 is an exact replica of Colt's Model 603. The US manufacturer designates it as M 603 K and marks it as follows:
- On the left: M 16 A1
  K00000
- On the right: Made in Korea under licence from Colt's, Hartford, CT. U.S.A.

Daewoo has manufactured its own derivatives of the M 16, which are known as K 1 and K 2 (or MAX-I and MAX-II).

Both have a light alloy body and work by blowback gas with a piston which activates the bolt; the cocking lever is on the right and angled upward.
- The K 1 has a telescoping buttstock with two rods.

Specifications	S. Korean K 1	S. Korean K 2
Caliber	5.56mm	5.56mm
Ammunition	5.56 x 45	5.56 x 45
Total length with buttstock extended	0.851 meter	0.990 meter
Total length with buttstock retracted	0.663 meter	0.736 meter
Barrel length	0.266 meter	0.457 meter
Weight without magazine	2.850kg	3.170kg
Magazine capacity	30 rounds	30 rounds
Rate of fire	700-900 rounds/minute	700-900 rounds/mn

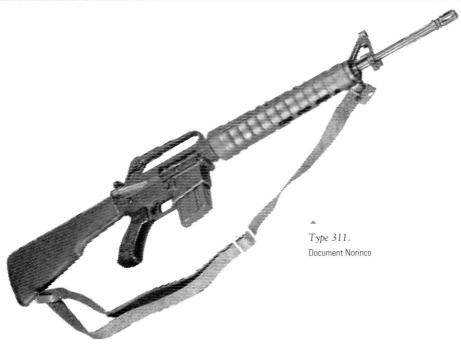

Type 311.
Document Norinco

K 1 Assault rifle with telescoping buttstock.
Document Daewoo

K 2 Assault rifle with swiveling buttstock.
Document Daewoo

SAR 80 Assault rifle.
Photo CIS

- The K 1 A1 is a short barreled carbine
- Le K 2 has a synthetic buttstock which can be swiveled sideways.

The Daewoo K series weapons are imported into the United States by Stoeger Arms.

TAIWAN

Taiwan manufactured the Type 65 rifle, which is an exact copy of the M 16. There is also a Type 68 rifle, based on the M 16 with a piston-operated gas cylinder.

We have seen in the preceding chapter that the M 16 and its derivatives have been produced under license.

But ever since the weapon was first introduced, manufacturers have produced copies to their heart's content, to such an extent that the copies and variations now available are far too numerous to count.

Here as elsewhere, the best run alongside the worst.

Some manufacturers offer complete weapons, some self-assembly kits and yet others roughly made parts (body, mount) cast or forged, which have to be completely machine finished. It is beyond the capability of some manufacturers to make an M 16 to the proper standards with the equipment they have available.

Precision and fantasy run together. Alongside , regular matt black models are bizarre examples in vivid colors: pink and metallic blue vie with gold-plated parts or parts made of titanium or stainless steel.

A whole book could be written about the derivatives of the M 16 alone.

The American Spirit Arms Corp's carbine markings.
Photo Jean Huon

American Spirit Arms Corporation

A.S.A. (15001 .N Hayden Rd Suite 112, Scottsdale AZ 85242) is a competition weapons specialist. They manufacture weapons derived from the AR-15, bored for .223 Remington or .308 Winchester.

They are equipped with recessed breech casings with an inset cocking lever on the left hand side. They also have precision barrels.

The American Spirit Arms Corp. produces both .223 and .308 competition guns.
Photo Jean Huon

Bushmaster's range of military weapons.
Photo Jean Huon

Armalite Inc.

Before Eagle Arms became Armalite again (PO Box 299, Genesco, IL 61254) it marketed the EA-15E2 semi-automatic rifle derived from the M 16 A2.

It was equipped with a Match barrel and an improved firing mechanism.

It is now marketed in multiple versions: rifles or carbines with fixed or telescoping buttstocks and standard or specialized barrels.

The mount and the body are made of light alloy.

Armalite also sells a new AR-10 bored for .308 Winchester (7.62mm) or .243 Winchester.

Bushmaster

Quality Bushmaster Firearms (999 Roosevelt Trail, Windham, NE 04602) probably produces the greatest number of M 16 A2 bodies. These are used by other manufacturers.

Bushmaster also produces its own range of models covering both civilian and military weapons.

Among these, some are used to equip the Marine commandos in France.

The Bushmaster logo is a cobra.

Century Arms

Century International Arms (48 Lower Newton, St Albans, VT 05478) is a company which specializes in surplus weapons. Most notably, they offer reconstructed or reconditioned rifles under the name Centurion 15.

The Bushmaster logo.
Document Bushmaster

Defense Procurement Manufacturing Service

DPMS (13983 Industry Avenue, Becker, MN 55308) makes competition weapons and each model is individually tailored to the client's requirements. It is even possible to obtain weapons with stainless steel bodies and mounts. This is a measure of their high standards.

The EDGE, produced by RND.
Photo Mesa Sportsmen's Association

European Army Arms Co

E.A.A. Co. (KR, Spa LA) makes semi-automatic carbines which it markets as J-15. The mount and the body are of steel! It is certainly strong but it is very heavy.

Evolution USA

Evolution USA P.O. Box 154, White Bird (Idaho 83554), is an armorer which improves the AR-15, equips it with every conceivable accessory and personalizes it. The body can be metallic blue, sugar pink or fluorescent green!

Specific marks on first generation Olympic weapons.

JP Enterprise

JP is a customization specialist capable of taking an old Vietnam War surplus M 16 and turning it into a formidable piece of equipment. It is true that after its treatment there will not be much left of the original weapon!

Olympic Arms Carbine.
Photo Jean Huon

Knight's Manufacturing Company

KMC (77750 9th Street S.W., Vero Beach, FL 32968) makes semi-automatic .223 and .308 rifles to order for sportsmen and the military. For its most recent developments it has had the assistance of Gene Stoner himself.

The Patriot Pistol.
Photo Jean-Louis Courtois

An Olympic Arms AR-15
A3 customized in Germany
by Waffen Schumacher.
Photo Jean Huo

Les Baer Customs Inc.

Las Baers (29610 34th Avenue, Hillsdale, IL 61257) produce most of the parts for the M 16 A1 or the M 16 A2 and also numerous accessories. There is a vast number of combinations and a variety of applications (shooting, hunting, competition, crowd control).

Olympic Arms Inc.

Olympic Arms (620-626 Old Pacific Highway SE, Olympia, WA 98513) offers semi-automatic weapons based on the AR-15, competition weapons with barrels of specialist steel and a whole range of equipment to produce "à la carte" weapons.

The first series had a logo with the letters SGW in a circle surrounded by an octagon. It now uses a lion which is surprisingly like that used by French car manufacturer Peugeot.

The logo on recent Olympic Arms products is a lion.
Photo Jean Huon

Panther

With Panther there is no automation.

Their M 16 works by pump action, i.e. manual repetition by sliding the forepart.

Professional Ordnance

Drawing their inspiration from the new generation of M 16s with modular breech casing, Professional Ordnance Inc (1070 Metric Drive, Lake Havasu City, AZ 86403) developed a carbon fiber weapon with cylindrical handguard, independent piston and stainless steel barrel. This was named Carbon 15.

It is offered either as a rifle with fixed buttstock (Type 97) or a short-barreled pistol with no buttstock (Type 20).

RDN Manufacturing Inc.

RDN, in association with MESA Sportsmen's Association and other accessory manufacturers, produce a .308 precision rifle.

It has a specialized buttstock, a ventilated carbon fiber handguard, a titanium firing pin, etc.

Rocky Mountains Arms Inc;

RMA produce the Patriot, a compact short-barreled weapon with no buttstock.

Rock River Arms

In 2000, Rock River Arms (101 Noble Street, Cleveland, IL 61241) entered the field of AR-15 applications by producing rifles and carbines derived from the M 16 A2, but with barrels lacking flash suppressors.

The Carbon 15 from Professional Ordnance.
Photo Professionnal Ordnance

Waffenfabrik Bern

During the 1980s when it became necessary to find a replacement for the Stgw 57, the Swiss authorities asked SIG and W & F to produce a new assault rifle. SIG won the contract by proposing a derivative of the SG 543 bored for a 5.56 x 45 cartridge.

As for Waffenfabrik Bern, they offered a derivative of the M 16 firstly chambered for

specific ammunition: 5.6 x 48 and 6.45 x 48, and subsequently for 5.56 x 45.

Wilson Combat

Wilson Combat (2234 CR 719 Berryville, AR 72616) are specialists in the production of weapons for sportsmen and police marksmen. They produce precision weapons fitted with telescopic sight, a tubular carbon fiber handguard and a bipod stand.

The Eiger assault rifle from Switzerland.
Photo W + F Bern.

The M 16 and its derivatives in use around the World

The M 16 is used all over the world. Some countries have bought it direct from Colt, some have obtained it from the United States under military aid programs, others use derivatives or copies and finally some make use of second-hand weapons.

Argentina
• M 16 or derivative bought from Colt.

Australia
• XM 177 E2 (bought from Colt.)

Barbados
• M 16 A1.
• M 16 A2.

Belize
• M 16 A1 (Colt Model 613). 400 supplied by the United Kingdom.

Bolivia
• M 16 A1.

Brazil
• M 16 A1 (Colt Model 514). There are at least 500 in the Air Force and 1000 with the Police.

The Eiger assault rifle from Switzerland.
Photo Diemaco

• M 16 A2, used by the Presidential Guard. These weapons were bought from Colt.

Brunei
• M 16 A1 (Colt Model 613). About 3800 of this and the following model.
• M 16 A1 carbine (Colt Model 653).
• XM 177 E2 (Colt Model 639), at least 240.
• M 16 A1 HBAR (Colt Model 611). All these weapons were bought from Colt.

Burma
• with M 203 grenade launcher.

Cambodia
• M 16 A1, 180,972 units from 1970 to 1975.

At the time of the Kolwezi operation in 1979 French legionnaires recovered a number of M 16s.
Photo Képi Blanc

Markings on C 7 rifles in service in Canada.
Photo Diemaco

Nowadays the Israeli Army is equipped with M 16 A1 rifles or carbines.
Photo Tzahal (IDF)

Cameroon
- M 16 A1 (Colt Model 613), in the region of 2 800 units.

Canada
- AR-15, used by the R.C.M.P.
- Carbine M 16 A1.
- FC 7 Rifle.
- C 8 carbine, all manufactured by Diemaco.

Central African Republic
- M 16 A1 (not confirmed).

Chile
- M 16 A1 (Colt Model 613), 5 000 units between 1976-1977.
- M 16 A2, in service with the Marines Rifles. These weapons were bought from Colt.

China
- The People's Republic of China produced Model 311, a copy of the M 16 A1, the weapon being distributed by Norinco.

Colombia
- M 16 or derivative bought from Colt.

Costa Rica
- M 16 A1.
- Type 68, bought from Taiwan.

Denmark
- M 16 A1, used by the police before 1988.
- C 7, Denmark adopted the Diemaco-made Canadian version of the M 16 A2.

Dominican Republic
- 1060 units in 1982 and 5000 more later on. They are used by Presidential Guard and by cadets at the military academy.

Egypt
- M 16 A1, 40 for evaluation purposes in 1981.
- Other deliveries followed (supplied by Colt).

El Salvador
- M 16 A1, 11,886 in 1981-1982 given in military aid and 20,743 others acquired between 1982 and 1984.

This M 16 A1 is equipped with a barrel cooler and a 40mm M 203 grenade launcher, with an open sight alidade.
Photo Tzahal (IDF)

In Lebanon French troops met local units equipped with the M 16.
Photo Képi Blanc

Royal guards of the Principality of Monaco seen here with their M 16 A2's
Photo Principauté de Monaco

M 16 A 2's in service in Monaco equipped with the M 7 bayonet
Photo Principauté de Monaco

Ecuador
- M 16 A1 (Colt Model 653). 35,000 used by the special forces.

France
- M 16, several examples bought for experimentation purposes under the FAMAS tests.
- retrieved by the 2è REP (2nd Foreign Legion Parachute Regiment) following the Kolwezi Expedition in 1979; also from Lebanon.
- Several hundred of these, equipped with 40mm grenade launchers, are in service with the crack units of the COS (Special Operations Command).
- Most of these M 16 A2s were bought from Colt, others (in particular those of the Marine Commandos), came from Bushmaster.
- M 16 A2 Carbine, in service with other specialist units such as the 11è Choc (11th Shock Parachute Regiment - the armed wing of the French counter-espionage service).

Gabon
- M 16 A1 (Colt Model 613 & Model 653), 2000 were obtained.

Markings on C 7 rifles produced in Canada for Norway.
Photo Diemaco

Ghana
- M 16 A1 (Colt Model 613), in the region of 6000 units.

Greece
- M 16 A2, about 300 for special forces (supplied by Colt).

Grenada
- M 16 A1.

Guatemala
- M 16 A1, bought from Colt.

Markings on C 7s produced in Canada for the Netherlands.
Photo Diemaco

Markings on C 7s produced in Canada for the United Kingdom.
Photo Diemaco

Haiti
• M 16 A1, around 500 units.

Honduras
• M 16 A1 (Colt Model 613).
• M 16 A1 (Colt Model 653). Some 9500 in total.

Indonesia
• AR-15.
• M 16 A2, 80,000, delivered in several consignments.

Israel
• Although Israel Military Industries had developed the Galil, a 5.56mm assault rifle, it was considered that the M 16 A2 Carbine with telescoping buttstock and the Combat Optical Gunsight should in future be used to equip Tzahal (Israel Defence Forces), while the M 16 A1 should be used for the protection forces.

Italy
• Colt laid claim to the supply of the M 16 to the Italians. It was only a brief piece of business for them as the Italian armed forces had already adopted the Beretta AR 70.

Ivory Coast
• M 16 A1.

Jamaica
• M 16 A1 (Colt Model 613 & Model 653).

Jordan
• M 16 A2.

Kenya
• M 16 or derivatives supplied by Colt.

Laos
• M16 A1, 88,469 between 1968 and 1974.

Latvia
• M16 A1

Lebanon
• M 16 A1 (Colt Model 613). At least 117,400 delivered. They have a serial number preceded by the letters AL, the Lebanese cedar tree and an FIS monogram.

Liberia
• M 16 A1 (Colt Model 613).
• M 16 A1 HBAR.
• M 16 A2.

Lithuania
• M 16 A1, of US origin.

Lesotho
• M 16 A1 (Colt Model 613 & Model 653).

Propaganda photograph, posed for effect. The man in the foreground has no equipment and the shutter on the ejection port of his weapon is closed! The man behind is loaded like a pack mule, with bullet-proof vest, rucksack and an M 72 LRAC LAW. One wonders what good he can do here…
Author's collection

Malaysia
- M 16 A1 (Colt Model 613), 200,000 units.
- M 16 A1 (Colt Model 653), 5000 bought direct from Colt.

Maldives
- M 16 A1.

Mexico
- M 16 or derivatives bought from Colt.

Monaco
- M 16 A2, used by the Prince's Corps of Carabineers.

Morocco
- M 16 A1 (Colt Model 613 & Model 653).

Netherlands
- Geweer C-7, Canadian version of the M 16 A2.
- Karabijn C-8, carbine.
- Geweer C-7 A1, marksman's rifle with 3.5x telescopic sight.
- Loaw, machine gun version with heavy barrel. It was intended to acquire 33,400 weapons for ground troops, 5284 for the Navy, 12,000 for the Air Force and 1400 for the Police.

New Zealand
- New Zealand procured a few C 7 rifles from Diemaco before opting for the Steyr AUG.

Nicaragua
- M 16 A1 (Colt Model 613 & Model 653), in the region of 6000.

Nigeria
- M 16 derivatives supplied by Colt.

Norway
- Norway adopted the M 16 A2 produced under license by Diemaco of Canada.

Oman
- M 16 A1 (Colt Model 613), about 3000 used by the Sultan's Guard and the Omani special forces.

Palestine
- The various militias in the areas under the control of the Palestinian Authority use a variety of weapons, among which is the M 16 A1 in both rifle and carbine forms.

Panama
- M 16 A1 (Colt Model 613), some 2000.
- Type 65, a weapon of Chinese origin

South Vietnam used nearly a million M 16 A1s.
Author's collection

A sentry with an M 16 A1 stands guard at the royal palace in Bangkok. Close by (beyond this picture)is a guard post with more than twenty soldiers and one single 12.7mm machine gun on a carriage frame.

Photo Jean Huon

Papua-New Guinea
- M 16 A1.

Peru
- M 16 A1, for use by the Police.

Philippines
- After 72,000 M16 A1s had been delivered (bought in whole or in part from Colt), the weapon's production license was ceded to

Elisco Tool who ensured continued production for the local armed forces.

Poland
- M 16 A1, used by some special units and by frontier guards.

Qatar
- M 16 A1 (700).

Senegal
- M 16 (50).

Singapore
- After receiving 18,000 M 16s (Colt Model 614-S), Chartered Industries of Singapore undertook to produce the rifle to supply the local armed forces (150,000-180,000).
- M 16 A1 HBAR (Colt Model 611), 2300 in number.

Somalia
- M 16 A1 (3000).

South Africa
- M 16 A1, used by guard and security services.

South Korea
- M 16 A1. Colt delivered 26,810 before 1983. After that date the production license was transferred first to the Pusan Arsenal and then later to to the Daewoo corporation, who have produced 590,000.
- K 1, local copy of the M 16 A1.
- K 2, carbine version of the K 1.

Sri Lanka
- M 16 A1.
- M 16 A2 (Colt Model 723), 300 for used by Special Forces.

Taiwan
- M 16 A1 (Colt Model 613). A first consignment of 47,000 weapons was delivered by Colt before 1976.
- Type 65, local copy of the M 16.
- Type 68, derived from the M 16 with piston operated gas cylinder.

Thailand
- M 16 A1 (Colt Model 613). A first consignment of 47,000 weapons was delivered by Colt before 1976.
- Type 65, local copy of the M 16.
- Type 68, derived from the M 16 with piston operated gas cylinder.

Trinidad & Tobago
- M 16 A1. Around 100 were obtained for use by the Police.

This guard close to President Mobutu of Zaïre is equipped with an M 16.

Photo Képi Blanc

Tunisia
- M 16 A1.

Turkey
- M 16 A2. rifle and carbine used by the security forces. (Supplied by Colt)

Uganda
- M 16 A1.

United Arab Emirates
- M 16 A1 (Colt Model 613 & Model 653), about 500.
- M 16 A2 (Colt Model 703), 30 000.
- M 16 A2 (Colt Model 727), 20 000.

United Kingdom
- The British initially acquired from Colt 750 AR-15s of the first type with forked flash-

suppressors. Later, M 16s were observed in use by British troops operating in Northern Ireland.
- The Royal Marines and the SAS were supplied with Model 613 rifles and Model 653 carbines.
- UK troops also use M 16 A2s produced by Diemaco of Canada.

United States of America
- M 16 (Colt Model 604), used by the U.S. Air Force.
- M A1 A1 (Colt Model 603), ex XM 16 E1.
- XM 177 (Colt Commando Model 610).
- XM 177 E1 (Colt Commando Model 609).
- WM 177 E2 (Colt Commando Model 629).
- CAR-15.
- GAU-5/A/A (Colt Commando Model 649), U.S. Air Force version of the XM 177.
- GAU-5/A/B (Colt Commando Model 630), U.S. Air Force version of the XM 177 E1.
- GAU-5/P (Colt Commando Model 610).
- M 231, gun port weapon for Bradley M2 Infantry Fighting Vehicle.
- M 16 A1 Demil, Demilitarized version for training purposes.
- M 16 A2.
- M 4 Carbine

Uruguay
- M 16 A1, 600 recovered from Communist groups and originating from Vietnam.

Vatican
- The Papal Guard (or Swiss Guard) is equipped with the M 16.

Vietnam (North)
- After the US withdrawal, the North Vietnamese retrieved huge quantities of American weapons among which were numerous M 16 A1s. Some were sold by the Vietnamese to guerrilla fighters in Latin America via Cuba and East Germany.

Vietnam (South)
- During the war between north and south, from 1966 to 1975 the US supplied their southern allies with 943,989 M 16 A1s

Yemen
- M 16 A2.

Zaire
- M 16 A1, (20,000).
- M 16 A1 HBAR.

.22 Long Rifle conversions

Most modern armies use .22 Long Rifle carbines for firing instruction and training purposes.

These are sometimes obtained from makers or, more frequently by adapting existing weapons. This keeps the price down and allows the use of smaller firing ranges than those required by conventional munitions.

Since the nominal caliber of the M 16 is the same as that of the .22 Long Rifle it was clearly tempting to produce a conversion to allow training ammunition to be used in the weapon. Several outfits did just that.

Colt Conversion

The conversion offered by the weapon's maker consisted of a substitute for the breech. This was a tube containing a new bolt and had an ejection port on the right hand side.

A magazine for .22 Long Rifle cartridges was provided with the conversion.

This invention, by Harry A. Into and Richard L. Costello is covered by Patent No. 3.771.415 of November 13th 1973

Atchisson/MAC Conversion

The conversion brought out by Maxwell G Atchisson was patented on December 4th 1973 under No. 3.776.095.

It took the form of a hollow cylinder fitted with a positioning peg on the top section. This element constituted the breech case and had a right-hand ejection port.

The firing chamber in front of the tube was lengthened by a stamping in the shape of a .223 Remington case and ensured connection with the weapon's barrel.

The special magazine held 16 cartridges.

The Atchisson conversion is made by Military Armament Corporation of Washington. It allows single shot and volley fire.

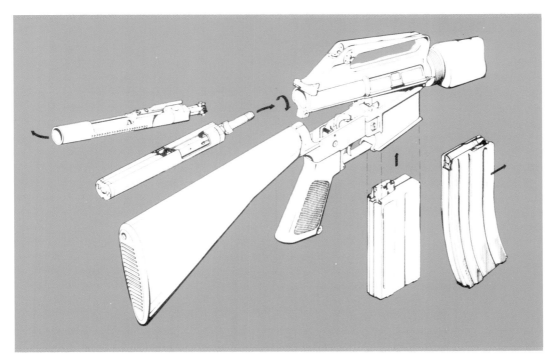

Conversion unit for the M 16 produced by Colt. It allows only single shot fire.
Document Colt

The Atchisson Conversion Mark III works equally well for single shot or volley. It is fed by 10 or 30 round magazines.

Using conversions makes it possible to keep the training costs lower as a single .223 Remington cartridge costs the same as twelve .22 Long Rifle cartridges.

Photo Bingham Ltd

Atchisson Mark III Conversion

Maxwell Atchisson produced a new conversion unit which was simpler to make because many of the parts were pressed.

It consisted of a yoke with two connected shells, the assembly being placed in the breech case. In front was the bolt proper, furnished with a recuperator spring on the top, sliding on the yoke.

A reducing tube is placed in the barrel chamber and this locks in place of the moving head and remains static during firing.

The Atchisson Mark III conversion is covered by Patent No. 4.169.329 of October 2nd 1979. It is marketed by Bingham Ltd, Norcross, Georgia.

M 261 Conversion

The conversion unit in use by the US Army was developed by the Maremont Corporation of Saco, Maine. Unlike the Colt and MAC versions, the breech does not operate within a tubular frame but directly in the weapon's breech block.

To achieve this, a fixed component is placed to the rear while the recuperator spring is above the conversion.

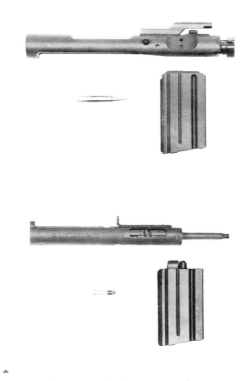

Comparison between standard equipment on the Atchisson/MAC conversion unit.

Weight of moving system: 325gm

Weight of 20-round magazine empty: 85gm

Weight of 20-round magazine charged: 320gm

Ammunition: .223 Remington

Weight of light breech: 368gm

Weight of 16-round magazine empty: 130gm

Weight of 16-round magazine charged: 185gm

Ammunition: .22 Long Rifle

Comparison between an M 16 with standard breech and with a conversion unit.

Photo Bingham Ltd

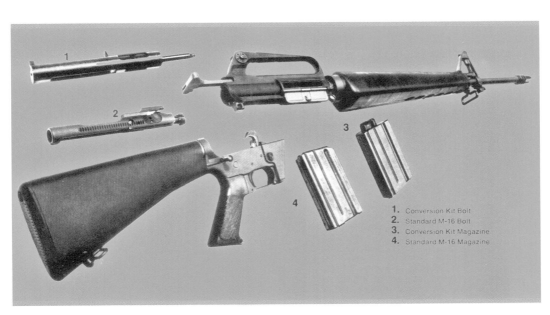

1. Conversion Kit Bolt
2. Standard M-16 Bolt
3. Conversion Kit Magazine
4. Standard M-16 Magazine

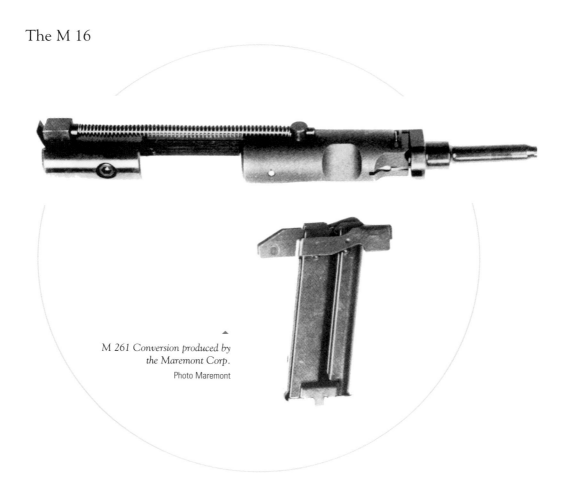

*M 261 Conversion produced by
the Maremont Corp.*
Photo Maremont

M 2 Conversion

The US Army has chosen a new conversion with a lighter M 2 breech block, firing a short range M 882 cartridge with plastic bullets. The .22 LR has been deliberately set aside with this equipment.

SCACS Conversion

This is an M 16 body on which are fitted:
  • a short barrel with a perforated forward half,
  • an Ingram machine pistol silencer,
  • an Atchisson/MAC conversion breech,
  • a 30-round .22 Long Rifle magazine,
  • a new sight.

This assembly is marketed by S.M.W. of Middleburg Heights, Ohio.

Canadian Conversion

Diemaco also produces a C 10 rifle, firing .22 Long Rifle ammunition. This weapon has more than 80% of its parts in common with the C 7 and can accommodate either single shot or volley fire.

Recreational use copies of the M 16

ARMI JAGER PRODUCTIONS

The Italian arms industry is well known for the excellence of its hunting guns and some manufacturers have specialized in the production of replicas of famous weapons. The most frequently made replicas are those of "Western" style revolvers and Winchester rifles. Applying this principle to the M 16, one Italian manufacturer produced a faithful copy as it is found in the .22 Long Rifle carbine.

This weapon was produced in 1971 and is known as the A.P.15. Three years later it was redesigned and renamed the A.P.74. Since then the basic model has had further adaptations.

These weapons are produced by Armi Jäger di Armando Piscetta, Loano, Italy.

Description

Despite the fact that the silhouette of these rifles is the same as that of the M 16, neither the A.P.15 nor the A.P.74 has a single piece which is interchangeable with the US weapon. It has a light alloy body and a dummy magazine mounted on the same unit as that of the carbine, and which is held in place by a transverse catch below. The safety catch is situated in the same place but the breech hammer block is offset forward and the trigger guard does not open. The breech case has a flat shutter which seals the ejection port.

The rims on the frame and the breech case of the Italian weapon project further than those on the M 16. The latter is anodized dark gray while the Italian copies are painted black.

A.P. 15 .22 Long Rifle Carbine made by
Armi Jäger in Italy.
Caliber: .22 Long Rifle
Total length: 0.960 meter
Barrel length: 0.515 meter
Weight: 3.100kg
Magazine capacity: 15-20 rounds
Photo Jean Huon

The A.P. 74.
Photo Jean Huon

: *Body of the A.P. 15 (right side)*
Photo Jean Huon

◄ *Body of the A.P. 74 (right side). Note the reinforcing ribs on the mount and the deflection regulating device on the rear sight.*
Photo Jean Huon

► *The A.P. 15 (left side).*
Photo Jean Huon

◄ *18-266 A.P. 74 (left side).*
Photo Jean Huon

The breech block is a simple cylinder of cadmium steel, secured by a screw on the top, and carries both the extractor and the firing pin. Firing is actuated by an internal hammer. It fires only single shots and cannot be adapted for volley firing.

▲

The muzzle brake on the A.P. 15
Photo Jean Huon

It is operated by an unfixed breech and has no gas cylinder.

The hand guard is positioned like that of the M 16 and is held in place level with the breech by a cup spring. It has no aluminum plate reinforcement.

The sight mount is of light alloy, treated in the same way as the frame. The dummy peg does not allow a bayonet to be attached. The forked muzzle brake has an external diameter of 22.5mm, which makes this impossible.

The A.P.15/A.P.74 gave birth to a plethora of weapons intended for recreational shooting and for use by police forces because they were available either as .22 Long Rifles or as 7.65 Brownings.

A.P. 74

This was simply a change of name for the A.P.15.

The two weapons are identical.

▲

The muzzle brake on the A.P. 74
Photo Jean Huon

Above: the bolt of the A.P. 15.
Below: that of the A.P. 74.
Photo Jean Huon

A.P. 74 with folding stock

On this model (initially designated A.P.-15P) the fixed plastic buttstock is replaced by a folding metal one.

The hand guard is plastic and three barrel lengths are available:
- Art. 320, 515mm barrel,
- Art. 321, 322mm barrel,
- Art. 322, 200mm barrel.

A.P. 74/L

A model similar to the standard A.P 74 but with buttstock, hand guard and pistol grip made of wood.

A. P. 74/I

Another short-barreled variant. The carrying handle has disappeared and the line of sight is lower. The lugged sight is also less prominent.

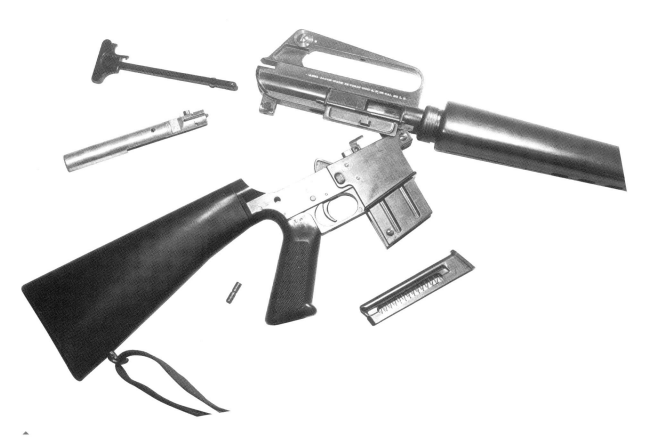

The A.P. 15 is disassembled in exactly the same way as the M 16.
Photo Jean Huon

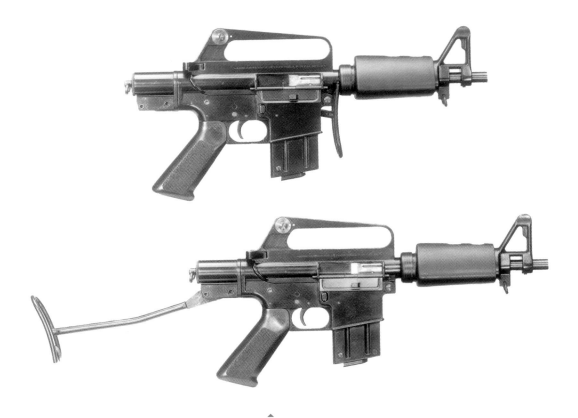

The short-barreled A.P. 74 with swivel buttstock was intended for police and guard forces.

Ammunition: .22 Long Rifle or 7.65mm Browning

Total length: 0.645 meter

Length with buttstock folded: 0.450 meter

Weight: 2.500kg

Magazine capacity: 15-20 rounds of .22 Long Rifle or 10-14 rounds of 7.65mm.

Photo Armi Jäger

The A.P.74/I can be fitted with a foldable metal buttstock or a fixed wooden one which is reminiscent of that of the UZI machine pistol.

A.P. 74/1 - 420

This is identical to the previous variant but has a longer barrel. It is available only with a fixed wooden buttstock.

A.P. 74/L carbine with wooden buttstock, handguard and pistol grip.

Ammunition: .22 Long Rifle or 7.65mm Browning

Photo Armi Jäger

Caliber: .22 Long Rifle or 7.65mm
Total length: 0.880 meter
Barrel length: 0.420 meter
Weight: 3.100kg
Photo Armi Jäger

A.P. 14/1 short-barreled carbine with wood trim. This model is found with either fixed or swivel buttstock.
Caliber: .22 Long Rifle or 7.65mm
Total length: 0.660 meter
Total length with buttstock folded: 0.450 meter
Barrel length: 0.200 meter
Weight: 2.800kg
Photo Armi Jäger

Much less successful than the A.P. 15, the Squires Bingham Carbine comes from the Philippines. The shape is vaguely similar to that of the US weapon but its conception is that of a classic .22 Long Rifle Carbine.
Photo Squires Bingham

SQUIRES BINGHAM

The firm of Squires Bingham Manufacturing. Company. Inc. (Paring, Marikina, Rival) in the Philippines produces a .22 L.R. copy of the M 16 but with less success than Armi Jaeger. It has a wooden buttstock, either plain or black painted.

LEITNER WISE

Leitner Wise Rifle Company (1033 North Fairfax Street, Suite 402, Alexandria, VA 22314) sells both .22 Long Rifle and .22 Magnum versions of the AR-15. The Magnums are offered either as rifles or carbines and one of them, the LW 15 .22, has been adopted for training US forces.

The Squires Bingham carbine comes with a wooden buttstock which may be natural or painted black.
Photo Jean Huon

This manufacturer also has a conversion unit (barrel-body) which can be mounted on the standard M 16. This is available as either a rifle or carbine M 4.

Leitner Wise also offers a weapon rebored for a 7.82 x 24 cartridge

PARKER HALE

The British company Parker Hale Ltd (Golden Hillock Road, Birmingham B11 2PZ) has, since 1999, offered a very successful copy of the M 16

A2, either as a rifle or a carbine. It fires only single shots and is fed by a ten-round magazine.

BALL REPLICAS

There exist many types of 'Air Soft Gun' replicas of the M 16 A1 and the XM 177, firing plastic balls propelled by compressed air.

These copies are very successful in the main. Their energy being less than 2 Joules, they are regarded more as toys than as weapons.

First generation cartridges

The M 16 and the M 16 A1 use the standard US 5.56mm cartridge with M 193 ball.

This ammunition is suitable for a 10-round metal strip magazine or for pouches of 20 cartridges.

- M 193 normal 5.56mm ball cartridge. Casing is brass, occasionally lacquered steel. Length 44.5mm. Coated, pointed bullet carrying a lead slug and weighing 3.56gm.
- M 196 tracer bullet cartridge. Pointed, flat-based projectile of coated lead with base tracer cup. It weighs 3.53gm and is identified by a red tip.
- M 195 propulsive cartridge. Without a bullet and now abandoned, it was used for firing 22mm finned grenades before the M 79 and M 203 came into service. Eight-fold star crimp.
- Blank salvo cartridge. Same form as M 195 but with five-fold star crimp.
- M 200 practice blank cartridge, without bullet. Eight-fold star crimp.
- M 197 test cartridge. Similar to the ordinary live cartridge but the base of the casing and the projectile are red. Case either brass or nickel-plated.
- Dummy cartridge. Vertically fluted casing. Not armed. Blind detonator shaft. Bullet sometimes double crimped. Casing brass or chemically darkened. Various other dummy cartridges exist (darkened unfluted casings, and totally black cartridges are just a couple of examples).

Ten M 193 standard cartridges in a strip magazine.
Photo Jean Huon

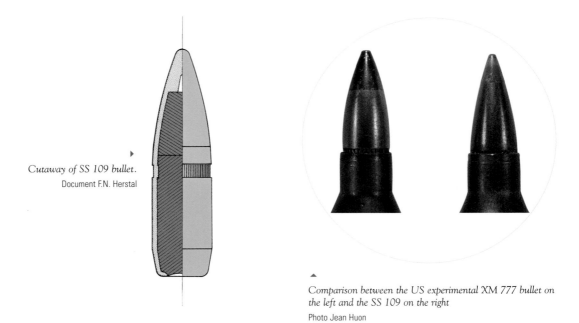

Cutaway of SS 109 bullet.
Document F.N. Herstal

Comparison between the US experimental XM 777 bullet on the left and the SS 109 on the right
Photo Jean Huon

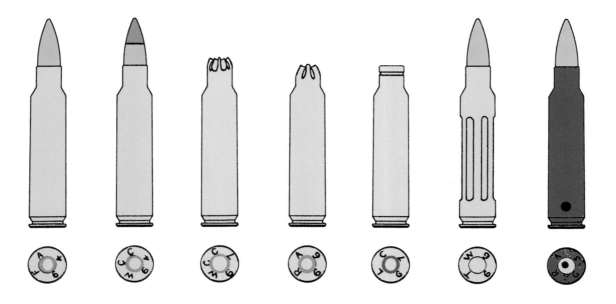

Principal 5.56 x 45 first-generation US regulation cartridges.

M 193 standard ball cartridge

M 196 tracer bullet (red top)

M 195 propulsive cartridge (8-fold star crimp)

Blank salvo cartridge (5-fold star crimp)

M 200 blank practice cartridge

Dummy cartridge with fluted brass case

Dummy cartridge, pierced and painted black

M 197 test cartridge with brass case; bullet and cap painted red

M 197 test cartridge; nickel plated brass case; bullet and cap painted purple

Fire Table

Weapons and ammunition used	Distance in meters	0	91	182	274	365	457	548
M 14	Velocity (m/s)	851	783	718	656	598	542	489
7.62mm NATO	Energy (kgm)	352	298	251	209	174	143	116
9.54 g ball	Camber (cm)	0	6	25	60	114	190	300
M 16 A1	Velocity	972	858	735	655	564	478	401
5.56mm M 193	Energy	171	133	98	77	57	41	29
3.59 g ball	Camber	0	5	20	51	100	176	290
M 16 A2	Velocity	927	839	754	675	601	531	465
5.56mm NATO M 855	Energy	175	143	103	82	65	51	39
4 g ball	Camber	0	5	22	53	102	175	275

The table above shows that the M 855 5.56mm NATO bullet with 4gm SS 109 ball outperforms the M 193 of the same caliber because its residual energy is greater at long distances as is its piercing capacity.

The trajectory of the two is very much the same.

Second generation cartridges

If the normal M 193 cartridge has the advantages of a flat trajectory, good mid-distance penetration and high wounding capacity, it does, however, possess several shortcomings. It is susceptible to light obstacles and has a tendency to disintegrate on impact. Its effective range is also limited.

Aware of this situation, the US developed a new standard live cartridge, the XM 777. The bullet had exactly the same outline as the M 193 and measured 19.18mm.

The XM 777's slug was bi-metallic which made it possible to move the center of gravity backward and improve stability. Weighing 3.53gm, this bullet was still capable of piercing a US helmet at 820 meters, but its coefficient of perforation and its long-distance stability were inferior to the Belgian SS 109.

The XM 777 is identified by its black tip.

The US also developed an experimental tracer bullet, the XM 778 (orange tip). Its ballistic qualities are close to those of the XM 777 and it was designed to be fired from a barrel with 305mm (12-inch) rifling such as on the M 16; the Belgian SS 109 works better with a 7-inch (180mm) rifled tube.

The development of the XM 777 and XM 778 was not pursued.

5.56mm NATO cartridges:
Standard SS 109 or M 855 ball
L 110 or M 856 tracer bullet.
Photo F.N. Herstal

The M 16

The US Army decided in the end to go along with the NATO choice, which was for the SS 109 and its derivatives:
- M 855 normal live cartridge (green tip)
- M 856 tracer bullet cartridge (red tip)
- M 882 reduced fire cartridge
- M 200 blank cartridge.

For more than thirty years the United States has poured millions of dollars into producing the ultimate infantry weapon.

Having sought in vain for a successor to the M 16 A1 by producing dart-firing or low-caliber projectile firing weapons, they turned to the manufacture of models firing combustible cartridges, without any greater success.

In some cases these prototypes were combined with grenade launchers, firstly 40mm caliber, then 30mm.

Finding it impossible to solve the problem of spontaneous ignition with combustible casings, it was decided to go back to conventional ammunition.

The principle of the OICW project.
Document U.S. Army

Some dart projectiles tested during the 1970s.
Photo Jean Huon

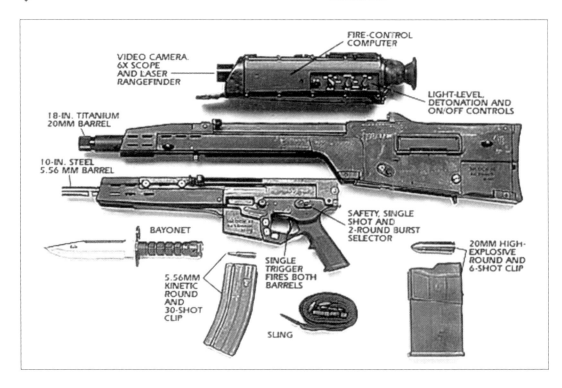

FIRE-CONTROL COMPUTER

VIDEO CAMERA. 6X SCOPE AND LASER RANGEFINDER

LIGHT-LEVEL, DETONATION AND ON/OFF CONTROLS

18-IN. TITANIUM 20MM BARREL

10-IN. STEEL 5.56 MM BARREL

SAFETY, SINGLE SHOT AND 2-ROUND BURST SELECTOR

BAYONET

SINGLE TRIGGER FIRES BOTH BARRELS

20MM HIGH-EXPLOSIVE ROUND AND 6-SHOT CLIP

5.56MM KINETIC ROUND AND 30-SHOT CLIP

SLING

The program envisages the production of two distinct weapons, capable of being used either separately or jointly:
- a light 5.56mm assault rifle firing conventional ammunition, both single shot and two-round bursts. In the latter case the rate of fire to be 850 rounds per minute
- a semi-automatic grenade launcher firing 20mm caliber explosive projectiles at an effective rate of 10 rounds/minute. These projectiles to be programmed to explode either on impact or 2.50 meters above a concealed enemy at a distance of 500 meters. The project envisages extending the effective range at 1000 meters.

▲

Colt's M 25 A2 and AA1.
Photo U.S. Army

At the time of writing (2002) the US is developing the OICW Program (*Objective Individual Combat Weapon*), which combines a conventional 5.56mm weapon with a 20mm automatic grenade launcher. The combination is completed by an infrared radiation sensor and offset sight mechanism. The concept was defined in 1994; several prototypes have been tested since 1996 and are in the course of development.

The test period should last until about 2004-2007 and these new weapons are expected to be in service by 2009.

▲

During the 1980s research concentrated on combustible ammunition.
Photo J. Huon

▶

The M 21 developed by HK and Alliant.
Photo U.S. Army

HK M 21

Heckler & Koch offer an HK 36 K modified to take an M 16 magazine clip. It is combined with a 20mm launcher developed by Alliant Technisystem

Colt M 25 A2

Colt offers a compact 5.56mm assault rifle with an automatic grenade launcher developed by the AAI Corporation.

F.N.

F.N. Herstal, the Belgian company, has also developed a specialist automatic weapon, which is combined with the AAI Corporation grenade launcher.

The prototype developed by F N.
Photo F.N. Herstal

OICW ammunition: conventional 5.56mm NATO cartridge, 20mm explosive tracer shell, 20mm practice shell.
Photo U.S. Army

The Vietnam Memorial in Washington.
Photo Jean Huon

EPILOGUE

The author had the privilege of meeting Gene Stoner in 1991, during the course of a dinner given by mutual friends.

We were able to discuss with him the history of the M 16 and the projects in which he had been involved over that period.

At the end of the evening I asked him, "Mr. Stoner, are you proud of the M 16?" He replied, "Sure, but have you've seen what they've done with my shooter…"

BIBLIOGRAPHY

SMALL ARMS OF THE WORLD – Joseph E. Smith & W.H.B. Smith – Stackpole Books – 1960 and successive editons

INTERNATIONAL ARMAMENT – George B. Johnson & Hans Bert Lockhoven – International Small Arms Publishers – 1963.

THE WORLD'S ASSAULT RIFLES – Daniel Musgrave & Thomas B. Nelson – T.B.N. Enterprises – 1967.

AR-15, M 16 AND M 16 A1 RIFLES – Donald Mc Lean – The Combat Bookshelf – 1968.

ARMALITE WEAPONS – Profile No. 22 (1973).

JANE'S INFANTRY WEAPONS – Jane's Publications – successive editons since 1975.

CONVERSION KIT M 261 - US Army (1978).

UN SIÈCLE D'ARMEMENT MONDIAL – Jean Huon – Éditions Crépin – Leblond -1976 -1981.

LE M 16 - Jean Huon – Éditions Crépin – Leblond -1983.

THE GREAT RIFLE CONTROVERSY – Edward C. Ezell – Stackpole Books – 1984.

U.S. RIFLE M 14 FROM JOHN GARAND TO THE M 21 - R. Blake Stevens – Collector Grade Publications -1983.

THE SPIW THE DEADLIEST WEAPON THAT NEVER WAS - R. Blake Stevens – Collector Grade Publications – 1985.

LES CARTOUCHES POUR FUSILS ET MITRAILLEUSES – Jean Huon – Amphora.

THE BLACK RIFLE - R. Blake Stevens & Edward C. Ezell – Collector Grade Publications -1987.

SMALL ARMS TO DAY – Clinton C. Ezell – Stackpole Books – 1988.

THE M 16 RIFLE AND ITS CARTRIDGE – David R. Hughes – Armory Publications – 1990.

DIE G 11 STORY – Wolfgang Seel – Journal Verlag – 1993.

FIREARMS – Wordsworth Editions – 1995.

THE UNITED STATES MARINE CORPS – Charles H. Cureton – Stackpole Books – 1984.

THE AR-15 COMPLETE OWNER'S GUIDE – Walt Kuleck & Scott Duff – 2000.

THE M 16/AR 15 RIFLE – Joe Poyer – North Cape Publications Inc. – 2000.

Technical Manuals

OPERATION AND PREVENTIVE MAINTENANCE OF THE M 16 A1 RIFLE – U.S. Army – 1969.

RIFLE 5.56 mm M 16 A2 - U.S. Marine Corps – 1984.

OPERATOR'S MANUAL FOR M 16 & M 16 A1 - U.S. Army – 1985.

U.S. MARINE CORPS TECHNICAL MANUAL – TM 05538C-23 & P/2 – 1984.

OPERATOR'S MANUAL FOR M 16 A2 - U.S. Army – 1986.

FIELD STRIPPING FOR THE M 16 A2 RIFLE – FMFM 0-9 – U.S. Marine Corps – 1995.

Magazines and Periodicals

ACTION GUNS
AMERICAN RIFLEMAN
CIBLES
COMBAT ARMS
DWJ
GAZETTE DES ARMES
GUILLAUME TELL
GUN DIGEST
L'AMATEUR D'ARMES
MEN AT ARMS
MILITARIA
RAIDS
SOLDIER OF FORTUNE
Etc.

Catalogs and Websites

Armalite
Bushmaster
Century Arms
Colt
Daewoo
Diemaco
DPMS
Elbits Computers
KMC
Les Baers
Olympic Arms
Orlite
Professionnal Ordnance
Ram-Line
Squires Bingham
Stopson
Etc.

Video

AR-15/M 16 - Rimfire Productions Inc. (1993).

The M 16

◄
A symbol of the Vietnam War taken up by the cinema.
Photo Jean Huon

◄
Macabre playing card left on the ground by US Special Forces after a mission.
Photo Jean Huon

◄
The Vietnam Commemorative Medal.
Photo Jean Huon

Acknowledgements

The author would like to thank all the people, companies and organizations that have so generously given of their time and who have all contributed to making this book possible.

M. le général directeur de la STAT
The Military Attaché of the Embassy of the United States in France
The Military Attaché of the Embassy of Israel in France
M. le Commandant de la Garde de son Altesse le Prince de Monaco
M. Alain Belladen de la société Stopson
M. Jean-Louis Courtois
Mr. Colin Doane
M. Michel Dumont
Mr. Edward C. Ezell
Mr. Gene Medlin
Mr. Thomas B. Nelson
M. Philippe Regenstreif
Mr. Eugene Stoner
Mr. Thomas, F. Swearengen
Mr. Donald, G. Thomas
Mr. William H. Woodin
Le Service Informations et Historique de la Légion Étrangère
The U. S. Army Information Service
The U. S. Marine Corps Information Service
The National Rifle Association of America.

Corporations:

Accuracy Systems Inc
Armalite
Assault Systems
Brunswick Corporation Defense
Colt Industries Firearms Division
Daewoo
Diemaco
Fabrique Nationale Herstal S.A.
Future Industries
Heckler & Koch GmbH
Interdynamic Forsknings AB
Laser Products Corporation
Military Armament Corporation
Orlite Engineering Co.
Standard Equipment Company.
Stopson.

Insignia of the 1st Cavalry Division (Airborne)
Photo Jean Huon